Understanding Short-Term Mission

A Guide for Leaders and Participants

JULIE LUPIEN

From Mission to Mission

A Resource for Mission and Transition

Our Mission

From Mission to Mission assists people in the preparation and processing of their cross-cultural, ministerial, and life transitions to continue their Christian call to mission.

This guide was written to provide practical support to those involved in short-term mission. I am grateful to all those who helped to make this guide the valuable resource it is, especially:

The School Sisters of Notre Dame, Mankato Province and all of our generous donors.

My trusted collaborators and advisers:

Joyana Dvorak

Mary Franch

Maureen McNamee

Anna Marie Reha, SSND

Matt Rousso

Michelle A. Scheidt

These gifted contributors who offer their wisdom for the good of mission:

Amor en Acción

Peter Fenelon

Rosanne Fischer

Christine Garcia, SSND

Judy Gomila, MSC

Mike Haasl

Sharon Horace, DC

Kim Lamberty

Darcy O'Hara

Matt Rousso

Michelle A. Scheidt

Published by **From Mission to Mission**, Longmont, Colorado. All rights reserved.
No part of this publication may be reproduced in any format without prior consent of the publisher.

Understanding Short-Term Mission: A Guide for Leaders and Participants
    by Julie Lupien
ISBN 978-0-9983160-4-8
Second edition copyright ©2017 by **From Mission to Mission** Society
Originally published as *What About Short-Term Mission?*
First edition copyright © 2006 by **From Mission to Mission** Society

Understanding Short-Term Mission

A Guide for Leaders and Participants

This book is published by the nonprofit organization **From Mission to Mission**.

In 1980 **From Mission to Mission** was created to offer support to returning missioners and volunteers as they deal with the unique transition of re-entry. As missioners ourselves, we understand the situations and life struggles experienced in mission that are virtually unknown here at home. We know the challenge of returning to a place you once called home and seeing it with a new vision that has been shaped by your experience in another culture. We also share the struggle to be faithful to the values, attitudes, and insights acquired during the cross-cultural experience. **From Mission to Mission** seeks to help returned missioners and volunteers live mission here in their home culture, in a way that honors those to whom they have said goodbye.

From Mission to Mission aims to offer support for all returning missioners and volunteers, no matter from where they return, or for how long they have served. This includes:

· Lay missioners and volunteers, religious sisters, priests and brothers, diocesan priests;

· Those who have served from a few days to those who have served for decades;

· International and domestic missioners and volunteers.

We offer publications, workshops, consultations, and other resources; see page 97 for details. **From Mission to Mission** is available to assist you at any time by phone, Skype, email, or in person with issues that arise related to trauma, whether you are an individual volunteer or missioner, a family or community member, the leader of an organization or community. Wherever you are in your mission journey, please contact us if you need support related to any aspect of re-entry.

—**From Mission to Mission**

From Mission
to Mission

missiontomission.org

This book is dedicated to those who loved and accepted me when I stepped from my comfort zone into their culture. I am especially grateful for:

The students of Nyatate Secondary School (Zimbabwe) and their families—for teaching me about faith, hospitality, and generosity that says if you have anything, you have enough to share. I am the person I am today because of you. May those students who have died from AIDS rest in God's arms.

Beulah (St. Kitts)—for teaching me everyday about life, faithfulness, joy, hope, family ... for EVERYTHING!

"Because I knew you, I have been changed for good" (from the song "For Good," from the musical *Wicked*).

Table of Contents

Table of Contents

Table of Contents

Introduction

Mission is not realized in a week or a month. Short-term mission experiences are pieces of a lifetime of mission and service. Short-term mission experiences provide opportunities for us to experience God's presence in ways that would never happen if we stayed home. Our experiences outside of our comfort zone, with God's people in other cultures or with people who struggle to survive, strengthen and transform us so we can continue to live mission wherever we are and whenever we go.

Each year, more and more Christians participate in short-term mission or immersion experiences through parish twinning, medical missions, alternative spring break, and parish or diocesan mission trips. These experiences last from a week to a number of months. Some go to places not far from home, while some travel to other countries. No matter how far you go, the important thing is to do all you can to make it the best possible experience it can be for all involved. Quality experiences do not just happen—they require a commitment to preparation and reflection. The purpose of this guide is to help you do just that, prepare and reflect.

This guide was written for both the participants of short-term experiences and for the leaders. It was written to help you go beyond "what to pack" and to focus on the meaning of the experience. The goal is to help you to understand the very important concept of mission and how to live it well in a short-term context.

This guide begins with Understanding Mission. We look at What is Mission? by exploring the mission of Jesus found in Scripture, the different elements of evangelization and by looking at four components of mission that are especially important in a short-term context—openness, presence, transformation, solidarity. Understanding Mission also includes an introduction to the Missioning Process—preparation, insertion, return—or, our purpose before, during, and after the experience itself.

It is wonderful to see how many people, motivated by their faith and concern for others, participate in short-term mission experiences. Unfortunately, lack of preparation or understanding can negatively affect the experience and even those we go to accompany. For advice on how to understand the "big picture" of short-term mission, we asked experienced leaders in short-term mission to share their wisdom in What Does Experience Tell Us?

Leaders of short-term experiences have a great deal of responsibility. Practicalities for Leaders lists what needs to be dealt with during the entirety of the experience. This includes details for each step of the Missioning Process. Because God calls us to mission and to be leaders, we look at Discernment for both participants and leaders. And because the focus of the experience is the people where we go, we include information on Crossing Cultures and how to approach people of another culture with sensitivity and openness.

The final section of this guide, Tool Kit for Reflection, is provided to assist you with ideas and activities that can be used during each phase of the Missioning Process.

Thank you for your willingness to share your life with others and for letting others touch yours. God be with you on this very special journey.

—**Julie Lupien**, Executive Director, **From Mission to Mission**

CHAPTER 1:
Understanding Mission

What Is Mission?

What a big question this is! Since the first Christian community, followers of Jesus have grappled with this question. Defining mission is not easy; there is no single definition. Over time, our understanding of mission has changed. What is important for each Christian today is to discover the answer to this question and to live it. This section explores different aspects of mission and then focuses more specifically on mission in a short-term context. We begin with a simple definition.

Mission is bringing about the realm of God. It is a commitment to transform our world into the world that God wants for each of us. Called through our baptism to live as Jesus lived, we become the instruments through which God works to make this possible. We have been chosen to bring love, hope, reconciliation, healing—the Good News—to all people, especially to those on the margins, just as Jesus did in his day.

To understand mission, we look to Jesus, for it is his mission that we now share. We turn to Scripture to learn about mission through the words and actions of Jesus. The following passages highlight the direction where Jesus points us if we are to continue his mission.

First, we see where Jesus himself was sent.

> *The Spirit of our God is upon me, because the Most High has anointed me. God has sent me to preach the good news to the poor, to proclaim liberty to those held captive ... and to proclaim the acceptable year our God's favor. (Lk 4:18-19; Mk 1:15, 38)*

Jesus taught by word and example what it means to be about mission.

> *I give you a new commandment, that you love one another. Just as I have loved you, you also should love one another ... (Jn 13:34).*

> *For I have sent them into the world as you sent me into the world ... May they all be one as you Father are in me and I am in you. May they be one in us (Jn 17:18-21).*

> *For I was hungry...thirsty...a stranger ... naked...ill...in prison ... Amen, I say to you, whatever you did for one of these least ones, you did for me ... (Mt 25:31-46).*

Then we have the missionary mandate from Jesus to proclaim his Gospel.

> *Go therefore and make disciples of all nations ... and remember, I am with you always to the end of the age (Mt 28:18-20, Mk 16:15-18; Lk 24:46-49; Jn 20:21-23).*

Jesus crossed cultural boundaries to speak to the Samaritan woman at the well. Not only is she transformed by meeting Jesus, but her sharing of the story of this encounter leads to the transformation of others who tell her:

> *It is no longer because of what you said that we believe, for we have heard for ourselves, and we know that this is truly the Savior of the world (Jn 4:1-42).*

Finally, Jesus Christ sent the Spirit to continue inspiring his Church in his final words before his ascension,

> *You will receive power when the Holy Spirit has come upon you; and you will be my witnesses in Jerusalem, in all Judea and Samaria, and to the ends of the earth (Acts 1:8).*

Jesus is our partner and model for living mission. With his words and actions in mind, we seek to understand what mission means in our own lives. What do we understand about mission?

Mission is About Evangelization.

Because evangelization is interpreted by some Christian groups as proselytizing, others feel uncomfortable with the concept of evangelization and choose to focus only on service. Doing as Jesus did is to evangelize, so it is important for us to understand what evangelization means and claim it as part of who we are. When getting to know another, we share who we are. If we are people of faith, we share who God is for us with those with whom we are in relationship. Evangelization is witness, proclamation, dialogue, peace, and justice. Let's look at each of these aspects more closely.

Witness: When we witness, we live what we believe. Jesus Christ is present when we live as he taught us to live. When others see our faith in action, whether it is how we show care to others, in the ways we go about our work, how we treat our neighbor or a stranger, or in our celebration and worship, it gives them an understanding of what the Gospel means. In time, others may question us about the way we live, which gives us the opportunity to proclaim our faith.

Proclamation: When we proclaim, we share the "Good News" of God's unconditional love for us, the life and teaching of Jesus and how the Spirit is with us and continues to guide us. Our proclamation is not to change another, but to share who we are. In our sharing we proclaim sensitively and respectfully what we have experienced and know to be true about the Good News in our lives. When we share our faith respectfully, it invites others to share who they are, in dialogue.

Dialogue: When we dialogue with others we engage in a mutual sharing of the God of our lives, in a way that leads to a deeper understanding of who God is for each of us. Dialogue is an opportunity to get to know another through examining questions of life and faith. Dialogue is not debate, but a way for each to learn more about God and Jesus and become more faithful to our own beliefs. When conditions do not make dialogue possible and conflict, tension, and violence are present, we are called to be peacemakers.

Peace: When we are peacemakers, we believe and proclaim that God can bring healing and reconciliation to any situation. Peacemaking is a stance and an activity. We work towards conversion to acceptance and respect of differences in our own lives. We take the stance that peace is possible in places where it seems hopeless. We are willing to be a peaceful presence in situations where violence, conflict, hatred, and forms of discrimination are present. Through prayer and action, we do what we can to encourage and support efforts towards reconciliation. As peacemakers we must consider the quote from Pope Paul VI, "If we want peace we must work for justice."

Justice: When we seek justice for all, we are actively involved in living the Good News of Jesus Christ which is to liberate the oppressed, set the captives free, protect the stranger, raise up those who are bowed down. This mandate of Jesus calls us to live justly by treating all people with dignity and respect and to work to eliminate the underlying causes of the suffering and oppression of God's people.

What Else Do We Know About Mission?

All Christians are called to mission through baptism. We have been anointed as members of the Body of Christ and are commissioned (co-missioned) to walk always as children of the light and to keep the flame of faith alive in our hearts. The mission of Jesus is our mission; it is not optional. Each of us is to discern how to live this mission in a way that fits who we are and the gifts God has given us. Jesus Christ is present in our world today through each of us.

We go and do what Jesus did. We go to serve, to be his witness, and to proclaim the Good News. We make our way to those who are poor, oppressed, rejected, lonely, sick, in prison, trapped in violence … who are in need of God's love and touch. Like Jesus, we are present to others; we listen to their stories, and we respond with love and care. We serve wherever we are and build mutual relationships with those we meet. Together we bring hope to our world.

Jesus calls us to GO! To follow Jesus we must leave what is known and comfortable and move to the unfamiliar, to the margins. The "margins" can be in our own communities or the "ends of the earth." It is not the number of miles we go, it is the willingness to go where we are called.

We GO for the length of time that fits who we are and the reality of our lives. The face of mission looks like all of us. We are women, men, children, religious, and lay, serving for decades, a couple of years or for a week, in our own neighborhoods or across the globe. It is important to acknowledge that short-term mission IS mission. Short-term mission experiences are one step in a lifetime commitment to mission, service, justice, and peace.

More and more Christians are coming to understand mission through a short-term mission or immersion experience. What has been written here so far is true for all those living their call to mission. The short-term experience is unique since it lasts for days and weeks versus years and lifetimes. The following components are true in mission, long-term or short-term. They are particularly important in a short-term experience. Short-term mission has four components—Openness, Presence, Transformation, and Solidarity.

What is Mission About in a Short-Term Context?

Openness: For God to truly touch our hearts, we must be open.

- We are *open* to God's call. We accept our responsibility to be the hands and feet of Jesus in our world today and not just when it is convenient or when we get credit for doing so.

- We are *open* to go where God calls us. Sometimes mission groups are asked to be involved in projects that may not be that exciting to us or seem that important. Mission is not just about glamorous accomplishments; it is about saying YES, doing our best, expecting no thanks in return.

- We are *open* to receiving from those whom we are called to serve. Mission is mutual. Those we meet offer us their faith, gifts, and hospitality. To receive is to honor them.

- We are *open* to learning. Mission experiences provide opportunities to learn about God, God's people, justice, our own country, and how its policies impact the world. We also learn a lot about ourselves. We meet our sisters and brothers face-to-face so that we understand them better and how our lives are interconnected.

- We are *open* to the risk of moving out of our comfort zone to meet Jesus Christ in the people to whom we go. We go where our eyes, ears, arms, and hearts are wide open, where we are poor, powerless, and dependent on others, where we do not have all the answers. We are humbled by others' hospitality, generosity, simplicity, and faith.

- We are *open* to being changed forever by our mission experience. When the God in me meets the God in you, we will never be the same!

Presence: Mission is God working through ME and YOU.

- Mission is about sharing who we are more than what we do. Being present to another is the most important thing we have to offer. God calls us to share our unique personalities, abilities, perspectives, and faith.

- Mission is about *being* rather than *doing*. We do not go to be so busy with work that we miss the people we go to be with. We do not go to complete lists of projects; we go to demonstrate and receive the love of Jesus Christ with those we meet.

- Mission is *being with* people rather than *doing for* them. We do not go to solve anyone's problems. We go to be with them, bringing the hope of our faith. Jean Vanier says, "To love someone is not first of all to do things for them, but to reveal to them their beauty and value, to say to them through our attitude: 'You are beautiful. You are important.' " And we allow others to say the same to us.

- Mission is communicating our love and concern across language barriers and cultural differences. Our presence says, "I care about you, and I will remember you." Creating a connection with others is the most important thing that happens in mission experiences. Long after we are gone, the work may be forgotten, but the memory of holding a hand, singing together, or communicating without a common language will last forever.

Transformation: God calls us to a change of heart.

- Transformation comes through mission. One interpretation of the word mission is conversion. But, we do not go to convert others; when we do go, we experience our own conversion and transformation.

- "Transformation comes when something inside us shifts and, despite ourselves, we find that we are no longer the person we used to be .... Then we know with certainty that God is working in our soul" (Joan Chittister OSB).

- Transformation is a gift from God. We trust that God will work through our mission experience in a way that will also transform the lives of those we meet.

- Transformation happens when we are open and present to God's people and the realities of their lives. Our immersion with the poor can lead us to examine our feelings, attitudes, and beliefs, and to surface questions about our own lifestyle, country, church, the poor, and the future. Through this experience God touches our hearts so we live differently, to help bring about God's realm on earth.

- Transformation requires prayer, reflection, and integration. Transformation does not just happen. We need to take time to look at our experience, pray about our experience, and let God speak to us through our experience. Reflection helps us to see how our beliefs, values, and vision have been transformed by the experience and how we might live differently by integrating this new understanding.

Solidarity: When one of God's children hurts, we all hurt.

- Solidarity is remaining faithful to the learning and values that have become important because of our experience. Our life circumstances may not allow us to "live" side-by-side, in solidarity with those we meet in mission. Our focus becomes living at home in a way that honors those we met during our experience. We bring them back in our hearts and minds and allow them to influence our choices and actions.

- Solidarity moves us to advocate on behalf of those we meet in mission and the issues that affect their lives. Perhaps the most important thing we can do for those we meet is to be a bridge to this culture that has so much influence in the world. Our story may be the only realistic perspective our listeners have of these people and this place. Our relationship continues when we pray, advocate, and act on their behalf.

- Solidarity impacts our lifestyle. Where we invest our time, energy, and resources affects others. When we live in solidarity, we truly live as one human family, knowing that *when one hurts, we all hurt*.

- Solidarity leads us to the realm of God.

What is mission? is an important question. Just as throughout Christian history it has been discussed and studied, has grown and changed, we need to continue to reflect on the meaning of mission. Whether through scripture, church documents, theologians, or our own experience, may our reflection always lead us to better understand how to live the mission of God on Earth.

Reflection Questions

Which scripture passages best describe your understanding of mission? Which passage stretches your understanding of mission?

_____

_____

_____

_____

How do you define evangelization? How have you demonstrated witness, proclamation, dialogue, peace, and justice in your life?

_____

_____

_____

What do you find challenging about openness, presence, transformation, and solidarity? Why? What comes naturally for you? Why?

_____

_____

_____

What are ways that mutuality might be demonstrated in a short-term mission experience?

_____

_____

_____

How open are you to "receiving" from those you will meet in mission? What might someone have to offer you? What do you think you could learn?

_____

_____

_____

How does this challenge or support your understanding of mission?

_____

_____

_____

_____

_____

_____

The Missioning Process

The Missioning Process includes three distinct phases of each mission experience—*preparation*, *insertion*, and *return*. Every aspect, from planning and preparing, to the experience itself, and, even the return from the experience IS the mission experience. Each phase has a purpose and adds value to the entirety of the experience. If one of the phases is left out, it impacts the whole experience. Unfortunately, not giving each phase the attention it deserves can have negative consequences for the missioners or those we meet during the mission experience.

The purpose of the Missioning Process is to:

- Help us, individually and as a group, to offer our best to those we go to be with in mission;
- Help us be prepared to meet God's people with understanding, respect, and sensitivity;
- Help us build relationships that are mutual, empowering, and collaborative;
- Help us to integrate our experience so that it transforms us, as well as those we represent;
- Help us to continue to live mission wherever we are, mindful of our connection to our sisters and brothers around the world.

Preparation helps us offer our best to those we go to accompany. Our focus becomes clear. We learn about the people we will meet, including their history, culture, and the current reality. We learn how to be with them in a way that is respectful and sensitive. It is an honor to be a guest in someone's home; our time in preparation helps us to better understand this.

Unfortunately, many do little or nothing to prepare prior to going. It would be an injustice to both the participants of short-term experiences and to those who will receive us to go without preparation. First and foremost, our focus needs to be on the people we will meet. We need to know something about them and how to be with them. Being prepared is a sign of respect for them and shows that they are the focus, not us. Many participants will be exposed to situations and poverty never seen before. Preparation helps each person to be more present to the reality we will meet when we get to our site.

Insertion is the cross-cultural experience itself, when we meet God and God's people in ways we never could here at home. Just being there is not enough. To make the most of the experience, we continue to learn about the local people and area, reflect on all that is happening each day, and be present to each other in prayer and worship.

Prayer, reflection, and sharing on a daily basis are key components to making the mission experience more than just a trip. Mother Theresa said, "Before you go into the world to speak to people about God, go to prayer to speak to God about people." Prayer keeps us rooted in our purpose and connected to the One who sent us. Reflection keeps us in touch with our feelings, questions, and reactions to what we are seeing and learning about the culture and society. What is revealed during reflection will be the starting point after the experience is over. If we are part of a group experience, sharing with others provides opportunities to learn from each other and to support each other throughout the experience.

Return is when the experience we prepared for is over and reflection and integration become our focus. The experience does not end because we are home. It can live on in us if we want it to. This requires prayer, reflection, sharing, and making choices about how we will live differently because of the experience.

Giving time and effort to the return phase is often neglected, yet it is an integral and extremely important part of the mission experience and is essential for ongoing integration and transformation. Taking the time to continue to focus on the mission experience after your return is the difference between "what I did on my summer vacation" and a transformative experience. The key to integrating the values and lessons learned during the mission experience and living in solidarity with those we met there is reflection, reflection, reflection! As Tony Saddington, a leader in experiential learning wrote "Experience is not the best teacher. We learn nothing from experience. We only learn from reflection on our experience."

Because so many groups neglect or struggle with the return phase, a companion book was created by **From Mission to Mission** to go with this guide. *Remaining Faithful: A Guide for Reflecting on Short-Term Mission Experiences* is a manual for reflection, integration, and prayer after a short-term experience in another culture.

In Chapter 3 called *Practicalities for Leaders* beginning on page 43, there is a more detailed explanation of the Missioning Process as well as practical suggestions for what needs to be done during each phase.

NOTES:

_____

_____

_____

_____

_____

_____

_____

_____

_____

_____

_____

_____

_____

_____

_____

_____

_____

_____

_____

_____

_____

_____

Reflection Questions

What is your reaction to the statement, "If one of the phases is left out, it impacts the whole experience"?

_____

_____

_____

_____

_____

_____

What negative consequences might there be for the participants and for those we go to accompany if not enough attention is given to preparation, insertion, and return?

_____

_____

_____

_____

_____

_____

What order of priority do you give to the three phases of the Missioning Process—preparation, insertion, return? Why?

_____

_____

_____

_____

_____

_____

Which phase(s) do you need to develop?

_____

_____

_____

_____

What is your plan to assure that each phase is given attention?

_____

_____

_____

_____

_____

_____

NOTES:

CHAPTER 2:
Essays: Learning from Experience

The purpose of this guide is to help you understand mission and how to live it well in a short-term context. There is no single approach to offer. Instead, we challenge you to think beyond your group and your interests, to look at the "big picture" of mission. We include here the perspectives and words of wisdom from people experienced in the area of mission, especially short-term mission. Each was given the task to write about a specific aspect of mission and share with you what their years of experience have taught them. We hope the following essays will challenge you and your group to examine your own understanding and practice of mission.

Reflection Questions

After reading each essay, consider the following questions:

What is your reaction?

How does this support your understanding and practice of short-term mission?

How does this differ from your understanding and practice of short-term mission?

What is the challenge you and your group need to take from this essay?

What action will you take?

Mission Trips—Why Do We Go?
Seeking Solidarity With the Peoples of Other Lands

by Matt Rousso

During my years as director of the Maryknoll Mission Education Office in New Orleans, I have been privileged to work with a number of youth and adult mission education programs that have included mission trips to Guatemala, Nicaragua, Mexico, and the Texas/Mexico border from El Paso/Juarez to McAllen/Reynosa. The U.S. Bishops' document "Called to Global Solidarity," along with heart-wrenching stories and pictures and news of victims of natural disasters (Hurricane Mitch, flooding in Mexico or Bangladesh, earthquakes in Central America, etc.) have strongly contributed to the phenomenal growth in the number of groups going on short-term mission trips. Some people call these "Mission Exposure" trips; others refer to them as "Immersion Experiences," and some organizations bill them simply as "Third World Delegations." Most generically, they are referred to as "Mission Trips." Invariably, the first question that is asked by an interested participant is *"What are we going to do?"* Perhaps we should be asking instead, *"Why do we go?"*

Even those of us working in the promotion department of the Maryknoll Fathers and Brothers see such trips as an important strategy for mission education. But we must ask ourselves and enable others to ask themselves what is the context for going into mission for such a short moment—whether it be for the eight-day, the three week, or the one year experience?

That we are first concerned with *doing* when presented with the possibility of going on a mission trip is quite understandable. Our culture and spirituality have formed us from our earliest days to see our significance in terms of what we do, and our original theology of mission has taught us well that mission and ministry are about giving to and doing for the poor. Missioners have so often spoken of their "success" in terms of how much they have done, either spiritually or materially—whether it be the number of converts made, schools built, clinics established, teeth pulled, or operations performed, houses repaired, Bible classes taught, etc. It is only in recent years that we have begun to understand that our significance as persons comes not from what we do but from who we are; and our understanding of mission has begun to change from "doing for" to "being with." Donal Dorr says so poignantly in *Mission in Today's World* that, as we have begun to focus on the *recipients* of missionary activity and not on the *great work* and great gift of the missionaries, we have come to understand that "mission is not just a matter of *doing things for* people. It is first of all a matter of *being with* people, of listening to and sharing with them."

So it is that, in the first instance, going into mission is not to help others or to teach others. Rather, it is for nothing less than for the sake of conversion—but not the conversion of those to whom we go; it is for our own conversion! And this conversion has to do with a fundamental change in the way that I view my own life—what I do, what I have, who I count as friends, what questions I ask myself, what issues I pay attention to, who and what I give my allegiance to. Somehow, going into mission helps that conversion. Recently a nun friend of mine who has been in Haiti as a missioner said, "our viewpoint depends on our standpoint." Richard Rohr in his book *Simplicity* says that, like the blind man in the Gospel, we need to yearn to see anew. For this new sight, he says "You have to run with your own feet to some place you haven't been before—to a new place. You have to leave the world where you have everything under control. You have to leave the world where everybody likes you. You have to head into a world where you are poor and powerless. And there you will be converted, despite yourself." I often hear myself saying that mission trips are about creating an opening for seeing and listening and hearing in ways that we are not easily able to do at home.

On the other side of this need for conversion in our way of thinking, is the need for conversion to the poor and often oppressed peoples of the developing world, who are deeply in need of friends and advocates from developed nations. Here again we need to be careful in understanding that this is a new call—we are not being called to old-style paternalism or neo-colonialism. The best in liberation theology has made it quite clear that the poor must be free to be the subjects of their lives and not simply the objects of our sympathy. Isn't it quite significant that the U.S. Bishops used the word *solidarity* to call us to new global discipleship? As if to say that we are not simply called to offer our neighbor charity but to engage in deep solidarity. Bishop Pedro Casaldáliga in *Political Holiness* speaks of solidarity as political charity: "Only those who make the rights of brother and sister their duty, co-working liberation with them, can be said to act in solidarity." Solidarity thus understood is not for a week or a month while we are with them, but for after we return to our lives in our home country. On mission trips we enter into friendships with the poor which can move us to live differently, to act on their behalf with a certain passion for justice issues. Dorr explains that "by entering the world of deprived people one extends and deepens the experience of 'suffering with' those on the margins. And, by doing so, one comes to share not only their pain and struggle but also their hopes."

Many today believe that we live in an era that challenges us to develop a global spirituality—a spirituality that has at least four basic characteristics: First, a growing awareness of human rights and some initial understandings about human responsibilities to others; second, a recognition of the call to enter into solidarity and realize our interdependence with the poor, who are often poor because of oppression; third, a deeper relation to God's creation itself, Earth; and, fourth, a greater bonding with peoples of other cultures and faiths as we see the commonalities of faith and belief.

And so, it is out of these frames of reference that the Maryknoll Mission Education office understands the importance of sponsoring and accompanying youth and adults on Third World mission trips. It is why we go.

Matt Rousso is currently Director of the Maryknoll Mission Education Center in New Orleans, LA. Since 1991 Matt has been associated with the Maryknoll Missionaries, directing the Maryknoll Mission Education and Promotion Office in New Orleans. His mission experience includes serving in Ecuador and directing Third World mission experience programs in Central American countries (Nicaragua, Guatemala, Honduras and El Salvador).

The Spirituality and Practice of Accompaniment

by Kim Lamberty, DMin

"The Church will have to initiate everyone—priests, religious, and laity—into this 'art of accompaniment' which teaches us to remove our sandals before the sacred ground of the other."—Pope Francis

Much of contemporary literature on the ministry of spiritual direction describes the relationship as "spiritual accompaniment." Spiritual accompaniment has several core components (Louf: ix–39):

- It is based in relationship, companionship, and presence.
- It calls upon the accompanier to witness their faith to the accompanied.
- The accompanier recognizes God in the accompanied.
- The accompanier never imposes anything on the accompanied, because even if the accompanier believes she can improve things for the accompanied, God's grace can do more.
- Spiritual accompaniment proceeds based on dialogue and mutual respect between the accompanied and the accompanier.
- The purpose of spiritual accompaniment is to call forth the fullness of life in the accompanied.

Accompaniment is always mutual, so that in a true accompaniment relationship each accompanies the other.

The starting point for any ministry grounded in an accompaniment metaphor is the dignity of each human person, as created in God's image. This same accompaniment metaphor expresses my approach to global mission, and is marked by the same core components. Mission viewed as accompaniment means mission is grounded in transformative relationship which is a catalyst for bringing forth the fullness of life for the individuals, families, communities, and institutions involved. The metaphor presumes movement and seeks transformation. An accompaniment relationship is grounded in and animated by relationship with God.

In a United States context, global mission in the 21st Century is dominated by church-to-church partnerships; short-term mission trips sponsored by churches, dioceses, universities, high schools, and traditional mission institutes; and volunteer programs of one to three years. These phenomena have accompanied a decline in the numbers of lifelong missionaries who were living and working in overseas communities for decades. These partnerships, mission trips, and volunteer programs nearly always immerse themselves into extremely vulnerable communities, marked by extreme poverty and lack of access to the rights and services we take for granted in the United States.

What explains the large numbers of committed Christians dedicating themselves to these new forms of mission? In 1997, the United States Conference of Catholic Bishops called Catholics in the United States to global solidarity, asking us to address the plight of and seek fullness of life for the world's most vulnerable peoples. In addition to this call from the bishops, people in the United States are inundated by media images of remote villages suffering from malnutrition, violence, natural disasters, disease, or illiteracy, and seeing the suffering of an impoverished mass of people moves us into mission work. Furthermore, committed Christians care about our relationship with God; we believe that this relationship is fostered through following in the footsteps of Jesus, and we understand that Jesus responded to the needy and marginalized of his day. We get involved in mission work because we are trying to help, and we believe that we are closer to God in doing so.

If the point is to help, then we must ask ourselves if the work we are doing actually leads to transformation, to the fullness of life, not only in ourselves, but most especially in the communities that we immerse ourselves into. Brian Howell, in his study *Short-Term Mission*, calls the current forms of mission "plight-based ministry" (Howell, 213) that serves the needs of the sending churches but does not lead to meaningful transformation in the host communities. Success is seen not as addressing the disease of poverty, but rather in rendering service and returning personally changed as a result (Ibid, 187). The sending churches or institutions see the programs as answering the call to respond to the poor through service, and finding opportunities for personal growth for their own parishioners, thus meeting their own needs. The problem is that such programs frequently do not meet the needs of host communities, because rendering a short-term or one-time service can do more harm than good, impeding the host community's ability to take responsibility for its own development and community service projects.

In a short piece about the partnership relationship between the Catholic Church of Peru and the German Diocese of Freiburg, Peruvian theologian Gustavo Gutierrez suggests that in a healthy solidarity partnership everyone gives and everyone receives. In this way, partnership is a process of mutual recognition of the dignity of the other—and as such is more than just a mechanism for wealthier Catholics to give something. Gutierrez affirms the desire for material support on the part of the less fortunate partner, but only in a context of mutuality and equality (Gutierrez 1996:53–56). Furthermore, Gutierrez has this to say about mutuality:

> To recognize the dignity of every human being, to value them as the center of their own decision-making and as the agent of their own destiny, implies an understanding that eliminating unjust structures is not enough. It is necessary at the same time to esteem and to transform the person from the inside (Gutierrez 1996:54).

To esteem and transform the person from the inside means that the starting point is love, and love comes from relationship. Gutierrez is affirming that the partner with fewer material resources wants to be seen by the other in their full dignity as children of God, and thus recognized as an equal partner in the relationship. The problem with a model of mission based on rendering service is that the partner on the receiving end of the service may not be experienced as an equal partner in the relationship. This desire for recognition as equal partners, and as agents of their own destiny, seems to be a motivating factor for getting involved in a partnership, but requires a process of transformation within both partners.

The Haitian Conference of Catholic Bishops released a statement not long after the devastation of the 2010 earthquake that supports many of Gutierrez's observations. After thanking the world for the tremendous outpouring of material support, they go on to say:

> The Church itself embodies God's love and fulfills her mission by promoting the fullness of the human person, who stands at the center of a new Haiti. More than food and shelter; chapels and schools; clinics and convents, we aim to build up every Haitian man and woman in his or her totality: physically, intellectually, emotionally and spiritually. If our work does not involve the whole person and every person, it is not true development. This then is our goal: integral human development (CEH 2010: 3).

The bishops recognize that solutions for Haiti will only take place through collaboration with global Catholic Church partners, but affirm that, grounded in human dignity, Haitians must be the "protagonists in their own development" (CEH 2010:2).

Using an accompaniment metaphor means that mission in the 21st century cannot be framed as Christians simply rendering service to poor communities and returning changed as a result. Accompaniment means that mission is reframed as a *relationship* based in mutuality and dialogue that leads to the fullness of life for all parties. The love that we experience in our relationships gives us power and courage, and sometimes that is all we need to overcome suffering. Mission is thus grounded in the dignity of the human person and a recognition that we all need each other, and we all have gifts to offer the other. The fullness of life encompasses our spiritual lives, and it also includes our temporal well-being, such as access to basic needs like food, clean water, healthcare, and education. For communities suffering from poverty, short-term service will not change their situation. Accompanying communities so that they are able to change their own situation must become a core aim of mission, and mission must therefore be framed as such.

In *Evangelii Gaudium*, Pope Francis writes that wealthier Catholics must put the poor at the center if we are truly to make manifest the Kingdom of God. Putting the poor at the center means moving beyond just charitable aid that ensures subsistence living. Francis seeks the full participation and self-fulfillment of those who are poor so that they may become "artisans of their own destiny" (EG 190). In addition to real relationship between the poor and the non-poor, "this means education, access to health care, and above all employment, for it is through free, creative, participatory and mutually supportive labor that human beings express and enhance the dignity of their lives" (EG 192). Francis refers to this process of inclusion for those who are poor, which involves both solidarity (the wealthy renouncing some of their rights so that the poor may have more) and the option for the poor (the poor and the rich become as one), as "accompanying the poor on their path to liberation" (EG 199).

Concretely, what does accompaniment look like? In a previous article I described the core elements (Lamberty 2012: 188–191). A spirituality of accompaniment begins with recognition of the dignity of the self as well as the other as created in God's image. It is expressed in presence, relationship, community, and mutual service. Accompaniment can also be expressed in a gift of material resources to assist a suffering community in rebuilding its future. Jesus illustrates in John 21 that the most suitable kind of material gift would be one that aids the community in providing for itself; Jesus did not get up and fish for them. This is economic solidarity, where a community with resources assists in the long-term income-generation projects developed by the materially-poor community. This kind of gift respects the independence of the receiver and understands the receiver as ultimately being in charge of his or her own destiny.

Best practices in mission are grounded in the core elements of accompaniment described at the outset and include the following:

Learning the language, culture, and traditions of the other partner

Real relationship is possible only when the partners can communicate, and when each understands the context of the other. Even rudimentary attempts to communicate in the language of the other go a long way toward building trust in the relationship, because if I am learning your language, I am committed to you. Out of respect and love, we also need to understand the cultural norms and traditions of the other.

Praying for and with each other

Prayer not only binds us to God, it also binds us to each other. When we pray for another, we cement our relationship. When we pray together, we express our communion.

Regular and reciprocal visits that focus on relationship-building

Most people in the U.S. want to do something during their short-term mission trip. We want to teach something, to build something, to treat someone's illness. Our focus is on doing rather than being together, and usually the agenda is so packed we have little time to rest. Accompaniment will focus on activities that build relationship, respect, love, and trust. If possible, the trips should be reciprocal.

Partnership with the local church and institutions, leading to mutual and joint decision-making that respects the leadership and community processes of both partners

In a true partnership, each acknowledges the value of the other. Acknowledging the valued role and gifts of the other is the starting point for creating a structure and joint decision-making process that includes both partners. Creating a decision-making structure that includes members of the wider community, and not just the pastor, will assist in developing and maintaining local leadership. Local leadership reduces dependence on outside aid and ensures the future sustainability of the ministry, whatever it might be.

Assessing the success of the mission based on whether the capacity of the partner in the developing country to lead their own future development has been enhanced, and not on how many projects were completed

Ask: In what ways have we worked with the community to improve their capacity to pay their own teacher salaries? How have we strategized with the community to improve their local health care delivery system? How have we increased the ability of parents to provide nutritious food to their children? It is essential to our human dignity to provide for our own families. None of us wants to be permanently dependent on the charity of others to take care of ourselves or our families. If our starting point in reflecting on global mission is the dignity of the human person, then we must move beyond charity and begin to look at solutions that facilitate and enable the community to take responsibility for itself. The goal of the partnership should be to reduce and ultimately eliminate the need for outside help, except in the case of emergency.

Evaluating and then acting together to address the underlying structural causes of the injustices that have led to poverty for the partner in the developing country

Some of the structural causes of poverty are addressed in the movement from a charity-based model of intervention that leads to dependency, to a justice and sustainable development-based model that stresses local economic development as a solution to poverty. In addition, the U.S. partner has a special responsibility to address U.S. policies that may affect global poverty, either positively or negatively. U.S. partners can begin by educating themselves about policies that directly affect global poverty and violence.

The dignity of each human person, grounded in the first chapter of Genesis, provides the foundation of all Catholic moral theology and also provides the foundation for mission. In recognizing the dignity of each human person, we also recognize that poverty is a scandal on the body of Christ, and we experience our missional call to go beyond rendering short-term service which simply allows the status quo to continue, but rather to walk in solidarity with our vulnerable brothers and sisters. Walking in solidarity is another way to say accompaniment, an active presence, based in relationship, that helps communities to move beyond their suffering. Mission becomes the means for individuals and communities to transform their situation of extreme vulnerability to one that enjoys the fullness of the life that God has given to each of us.

Resources Cited

Conference Episcopaled'Haiti (CEH). Prot. No. CEH 224/10, *Message of the Haitian Episcopal Conference Gathered in Plenary Session with Invited Church Representatives*, September 21–22, 2010.

Pope Francis. *Evangelii Gaudium*. 2013. https://w2.vatican.va/content/francesco/en/apost_exhortations/documents/papa-francesco_esortazione-ap_20131124_evangelii-gaudium.html.

Gutiérrez, Gustavo. "Partnerschaft: Liberación de pobres y ricos." *10 AñosPartnerschaft Peru-Friburgo*. Pp. 53–56. Lima, Peru: ParroquiaAlemania, 1996.

Howell, Brian M. *Short-Term Mission: An Ethnography of Christian Travel Narrative and Experience*. Downer's Grove, IL: IV Press, 2012.

Lamberty, Kim. "Toward a Spirituality of Accompaniment in Solidarity Partnerships." *Missiology: An International Review*, vol. XI, no. 2, April 2012, pp. 181–193.

Louf, Andre. *Grace Can Do More: Spiritual Accompaniment and Spiritual Growth* (Kalamazoo, MI: Cistercian Publications) 2002.

United States Conference of Catholic Bishops (USCCB). *Called to Global Solidarity: International Challenges for US Parishes*. http://www.usccb.org/sdwp/international/globalsolidarity.shtml. 1997.

Dr. Kim Lamberty is the co-founder and president of Just Haiti, Inc., a faith-based coffee development program that partners with small-scale farmers in Haiti to provide technical and organizing assistance and to market their fair trade coffee in the United States. She is also director of university and mission engagement at Catholic Relief Services, where she oversees implementation of social justice, fair trade, and advocacy programs through CRS at college campuses across the United States. She is the author of a book and numerous articles on mission and development and a frequent conference and workshop presenter. She holds a Doctor of Ministry degree from Catholic Theological Union.

Culture, Encounter, and Love

by Rosanne Fischer

One of the first controversies in the nascent Christian Church, as recounted in Acts and Galatians, was the question of whether one had to follow the religious and cultural customs and laws of Judaism in order to participate in the Christian community. Paul, missioner to the Gentiles, thought, after his visit to Jerusalem, that this question had been answered with a resounding, "No!" But in the second chapter of Galatians, Paul publicly challenges Peter, who is succumbing to pressure from members of the Jewish community who still insist that Jewish laws and customs be followed. Paul writes, "We know that a person is not made just and holy by the observance of the Law but by faith in Christ Jesus. So we have believed in Christ Jesus that we may receive holiness from faith in Christ Jesus, and not from the practices of the Law, because the observance of Law does not make any mortal a friend of God" (Galatians 2:16). The controversy involving the following of specific laws and customs continues and takes multiple forms in the Christian Church today.

It is part of human nature to be most comfortable with what we are familiar with. The animal kingdom likely shares this propensity. Our experience has taught us what works for us and for our local communities, and we pass that on to our offspring. This is a good trait which keeps each new generation from having to learn everything anew. There is a beauty to this in the church as well, as we build up and rely upon the insights and revelations of the people who have lived before us, going back all the way to the time Jesus walked the Earth.

The challenge in this is that if there is one thing we know about our Creator, it is that God is always creating and making things new! As we encounter people of other cultures and religions, whether abroad or at home, our perceptions, understanding, and faith will be stretched and expanded, just as they were for the early Christians. This is a good thing, but it can also be uncomfortable. We see the world through the lens of our own experiences, customs, and practices, so things may seem strange when we encounter what is different. That is normal! But just as stretching our physical body adds new dimensions and ease of mobility to our lives, stretching our experience adds enriched understanding, comfortability, and depth to our lives.

Three essentials that help us in encounters with those who are different are: flexibility, humility and open-mindedness. These are qualities of true Love—the kind of love we experience in Christ, beautifully defined in 1 Corinthians 1:13: "Love is patient, kind, without envy. It is not boastful or arrogant. It is not ill-mannered nor does it insist on its own way. Love withstands anger and forgets offenses." St. Paul tells us that nothing we do— even giving up everything we own—has value, unless it is done in love.

We can study languages, cultures, and theology and have mountains of knowledge, all of which are important, but if we do not put on LOVE, it is all in vain. Love will lead us into right relationship with God and with others. The Spirit of Love helps us understand the diversity of gifts Paul writes about in 1 Corinthians 12: "The Spirit is revealed in each one with a gift which is also a service." Another translation: "To each is given the manifestation of the Spirit for the common good." Love is not a feeling; love is an *action*. Love is to be shared, or it is not love. The Spirit of God is revealed through our *actions* of love, through sharing the gift of love we have received. Equally important, *each one* receives gifts to be shared. God endows all human beings with gifts, and God is revealed when those gifts are put into action for the good of all.

In this regard, drawing from scripture and tradition, the Catholic Church proclaims the following values in its documents:

- Participation is as important, if not more important, than economic growth. The largest numbers of people are active at every level.

- All peoples and nations are full participants and the primary agents of their advancement, recognizing their own needs and identifying their own priorities.

- Cultural and spiritual values are respected and received as a contribution to humanity.

- Lifestyles, commercial patterns, and power structures which institutionalize injustice and undermine the common good are to be radically changed.

- Through collaboration, coordination and genuine dialogue, true progress is made.

Depending on how it is done, entering into encounter with others, and especially offering material resources, can contribute to or detract from human dignity. It can build relationships, empower others, and release gifts, or it can create disunity, competition, dependence, and feelings of inferiority. Let us be mindful of the ways in which we approach others: with a spirit of humility and open-mindedness; with a listening ear eager to value and uphold the beauty, knowledge, and dignity of the other.

Pope Francis has written, "Work is a necessity, part of the meaning of life on this earth, a path to growth, human development and personal fulfillment. Helping the poor financially must always be a provisional solution in the face of pressing needs. The broader objective should always be to allow them a dignified life through work." All people desire to realize their full potential by contributing and sharing the gifts they have been given.

Encountering others who are different is messy. It requires living in tension between the way we do things and the way the other does them. We allow others to lead and allow ourselves to be stretched, challenged, and changed. We engage in analysis with others in order to identify and change policies and systems that institutionalize injustice and undermine the common good and people's ability to work. Engagement requires resiliency in order to pick ourselves up when we make mistakes, which we inevitably will. We engage with a spirit of mercy and reconciliation— a spirit of love—which holds our relationship through the trials and errors. We reflect upon and celebrate our unity in diversity—the sign of our Creator's Love—alive and well within us all.

Addendum: Characteristics of Healthy Faith Partnerships

- Broad-based involvement in both communities, including youth, elders, women, men, lay, ordained, religious, minority groups. Regular rotation of leadership.

- Ongoing dialogue, including clearly defined avenues of communication and travel of individuals and groups in both directions.

- Naming and recognition of gifts and needs within each congregation. Both communities reflect in an ongoing way on what they can contribute to the building of the relationship. Focus on spiritual and material development and empowerment of people in both communities.

- Jointly developed mission statement and periodic reflection and evaluation on whether the partnership is furthering the stated mission.

- Defined parameters of partner commitments, including timeline, people involved, and contribution of each partner. Emphasis in evaluation on open communication, enhancement of relationship, release of gifts, and building of trust.

- Ongoing formation for both partners, jointly when possible, in missiology, intercultural communication, scripture study, church documents.

- Reflection on their own culture by each community through the lens of their partner in order to define elements that run counter to Gospel values and the common good.

- Reflection upon systems and structures that foster injustice. Joint advocacy to effect change in those systems, structures, consumer patterns, etc, in order to create a more just and peaceful world.

- Observable difference in development of a global perspective in each partner community. The partnership is not inward-looking nor exclusive, but opens each partner community to greater universal compassion.

- Prayer and joyful celebration built into every aspect of the partnership. Group travel begins with prayer and orientation and concludes with a full day and night in silent retreat before returning home. Ongoing reflection built into the structure of the partnership to enhance integration and the growth of both partners.

Rosanne Fischer is a seeker who, since formative years in a large family home in inner city Minneapolis, has been learning how we thrive among diversity. Her study of History, Spanish, and Theology has contributed to her sense that the ideal state, authentic to our Trinitarian God, is unity in diversity. Her life has been enriched through encounter and relationship with diverse people in the United States, Mexico, Nicaragua, El Salvador, Venezuela, Kenya and South Sudan. Rosanne lives in Central Minnesota with her husband and has three adult children.

From Helping to Solidarity: A Reflection on Short Term Mission Trips as Part of Parish Twinning Relationships

by Mike Haasl

Most "sister parish" or "parish twinning" relationships are born of a beautiful impulse: to help other human beings who are struggling or more economically disadvantaged than themselves, to help those who are in need. It is an impulse that is generated in significant part by the Gospel mandate to love, especially as revealed in Matthew 25:31-46: "When I was hungry you gave me food ... "

The parish twinning phenomenon is a wonderful church movement that stands in sharp contrast to a sometimes isolated, apathetic, and protective U.S. culture which often promotes seeking security by looking inward and guarding one's every asset, rather than opening one's hands to others to share the gifts and resources with which one has been so richly blessed.

The true beauty and unique opportunity of parish twinning, however, goes far beyond "helping others." Sister parishes create the opportunity to build and engender real and even long-term relationships with people who are of another culture and often who are economically disenfranchised—and to begin to see and understand the world through their eyes. Gandhi once said that the best thing that you can do in your life is to get to know one poor person and to see the world through his or her eyes. Why? Because that experience will call into question many of the assumptions about the world that we are taught from a very young age, for example:

- that we somehow deserve our privileged place in the world;
- that people of the world ought do things the way we do them if they want to be better off;
- that if only people worked harder, they would have the opportunities that the average North American has;
- that the economic systems of the world are inherently good and in time will generate wealth for all.

Rather, when the poor person becomes our friend, we see their beauty and we can genuinely and experientially adopt the truth that we are all called to *oneness*, to become one Body in Christ. We can then more readily recognize that the current reality and the systems that created it are unacceptably unjust. We are beckoned to change those systems for the sake of the one we have come to know and love (and those others who share their same plight).

"Helping" can be done in ways that do not build those unique, real relationships. Sometimes helping can be a way of relieving the tension of the guilt that comes from the encounter of stark poverty when "I have so much superfluous stuff." Helping can be done out of a sense of pity, not a common sharing that occurs between people who really know and care about each other's whole being. When pity drives the relationship, the "other" becomes one-dimensional, not a whole person with gifts, joys, and love, but rather a need that *I need* to address to feel better about the situation. The poor, then, can become just an abstract object of our charity.

When I was a lay missioner in Venezuela, a missionary priest moved into our barrio, immediately setting out to build a large church structure and rectory. He was quick to provide funds for various needs in the community. Behind his back the local people referred to him as "dólar caminando," the walking dollar. He had virtually no true relationships among the people. He was essentially only seen as a source of funds. I would say that "helping" got in the way of relationship. I think that can be true also in many sister parish relationships.

The tragedy of this kind of relationship is that instead of oneness, there is still separation and all parties are left with the hidden sense of either superiority, control, and a sense of their power, or on the other side, a sense of inferiority and powerlessness. Twenty-five years ago in impoverished rural Kenya, I remember my white colleagues joking about the power of what they termed "musungu magic" (musungu is the Swahili term for white person), that is, how black Kenyans would give white people such special treatment compared with their black Kenyan brethren. From their childhood, black Kenyans had learned that whites were wealthier, more powerful and therefore, I believe, black Kenyans had (unconsciously) adopted an attitude that whites must be smarter, better, and superior than themselves.

In the U.S., good Christian children are taught that they must "help those poor people over there" but are often invited to do so in ways that unwittingly continue false unspoken pre-suppositions—that we have (and therefore must be better), and they don't (which must make them somehow inferior). This then leads to a pattern and attitude of one generous, superior party who "has it all together" giving to the other inferior, incapable party, who cannot make it without our intervention. These patterns don't lead us to oneness; rather, they perpetuate separateness. Although done with the best of intentions of helping others, they can foster dependency not wholeness.

Sister parishes and parish twinning relationships are an invitation to a whole different kind of relationship, whereby people from opposite sides of this historic divide come together, get to know one another more fully as human persons, the joys as well as the struggles, the gifts as well as the needs.

People on each side are seen as multi-dimensional, and partners are very curious and appreciate the various aspects of the things that shape the other—their history (personal, community, and national), their culture, their family life, their faith, and the varied cultural expressions of their faith.

Just as any friendship deepens when each side expresses their vulnerability and struggle, so do *both sides* of a sister parish relationship need to share their own pain and sorrow—so that the Holy Spirit can enter the vulnerable space and fuse the brokenness towards wholeness.

Like two people moving towards marriage, as relationships are established and trust is built, talk may turn toward hopes, goals, and ideas for building a lasting, healthy partnership. As with planning for marriage vows, both sides of the partnership should participate in putting together a Vision Statement and a Mission Statement, from which their various activities can be mutually developed.

Consequently, then, all parish twinning relationships should assess their activities—including their mission trips—with these questions:

- Is this mission trip or activity deepening our mutual relationship and understanding of one another? Are activities for deepening the relationship central and intentional or are they tangential to "getting something done"?
- Does the orientation for the mission trip include preparation in terms of learning about the history and culture, knowing a little about the persons in the community you will meet—their interests, their hopes for the encounter and for the partnership?

- Is this mission trip or activity exacerbating, or breaking down, the historic feelings of superiority and inferiority? Are the partners from the economically disadvantaged country participating fully in the planning, decision-making, and implementation of actions, or is it a one-sided "helping"?

- Is the mission trip or activity fostering a sustainable enhancement of quality of life as agreed upon by both partners? Has the potential negative impact on culture or social relationships been accounted for in regards to this mission trip or activity?

- Does the relationship or mission trip provide opportunity to reflect together on sacred scriptures and our faith, and so deepen our understanding of our faith as seen through the eyes of others?

- Is the relationship or mission trip helping both partners to learn about the root causes of the injustice affecting the disenfranchised community—the economic and political forces and systems which are at play? Is there opportunity to brainstorm ways to work together to address these systems of injustice?

By keeping these questions in front of both partners, and by honestly addressing the questions of power and historic attitudes of superiority and inferiority in the relationship, strong and healthy parish partnerships can be built and sustained. And a new world in the image of the reign of God, in what Pope John Paul II referred to as the globalization of solidarity, can be possible.

Mike Haasl is Global Solidarity Coordinator at the Center for Misson, Archdiocese of St. Paul-Minneapolis, where he works with parishes who are beginning or engaged in parish twinning relationships. Mike has been a coordinator of the Global Solidarity Partnership between the Archdiocese of St. Paul-Minneapolis and the Diocese of Kitui, Kenya. His mission experience includes a year in rural Kenya, three years in a barrio in Venezuela with his family, and parish social justice coordinator in a suburban parish where he steered the development of parish twinning relationship with a parish in rural Haiti.

Crossing Borders

by Judy Gomila, MSC

As a mission educator for the Archdiocese of New Orleans, I am constantly challenged to cross borders—and draw others with me. To sensitize the local church to the poverty in nearby countries, our office sponsors "immersions" for young adults, seminarians, medical personnel, families, catechists, and youth ministers. I have noticed that whether individuals participate in a border experience in Mexico, a catechetical Vacation Bible School in Belize, or a medical mission outreach in Nicaragua, the dynamics of these immersions are remarkably the same.

Typically, our missionaries arrive on-site and are overwhelmed by the poverty. They listen to the stories of the people—and experience the chasm between the lives of the indigenous folks and ours as U.S. citizens. Gradually, as our missionaries come to know the people they came to "help," they realize they are the ones being evangelized. Struck by the deep faith and spirit of community among the native people, they realize the locals are rich in ways far more valuable than material wealth. Distances between the missionaries and the others diminish as friendships develop and similarities are recognized. The foundation for genuine solidarity is laid.

These short-term mission opportunities abroad are certainly important because they help to bridge the gaps. Each experience moves our U.S. missionaries beyond themselves to get new insights into cultures, countries, and governments.

It has become clearer to me that borders among nations are not the only boundaries to be crossed. In many ways it is easier to feel solidarity with those at a distance than with people close at hand. In "hometown" USA we are often fearful, confused, angry, and prejudiced when confronted with the needs and demands of the marginalized. In response to people on our own turf, we Americans resort to the old "pull-yourself-up-by-your-boot-straps" adage.

The Gospel call to communion and solidarity is neither easy nor simple. We are challenged to address complex issues and situations—globally and in our own backyards. Everywhere there are networks of privilege, prejudice, and power so enmeshed in our systems and structures they are almost impossible to grasp.

Jesus espoused an inclusive vision. This spirituality requires us to:

- embrace our interconnectedness with the marginalized, wherever they are;
- defend the human rights of all our sisters and brothers;
- uncover common ground with peoples of all cultures and faiths;
- reverence all creation.

Eucharist is the sacrament of solidarity. It challenges us to keep crossing borders of all sorts, to recognize and receive "the holy" in the likely and unlikely. This is the call to be catholic—to be universally inclusive, to enflesh our belief that all of us form one body and are truly part of one another. This is the challenge—"to the ends of the earth" and at home—to make everyone welcome at the table of the Eucharist and the multiple public and private tables of our lives.

Judy Gomila, MSC, a Marianite Sister of Holy Cross, has been a Mission Educator for the Pontifical Mission Societies and the Archdiocese of New Orleans. Sr. Judy served in mission in the inner city, the bayou, and the Alaska bush.

The Bridge of Compassion—Domestic Service

by Darcy O'Hara and Sr. Sharon Horace, D.C.

Domestic service trips put forward their own kinds of gifts and challenges. Service at home allows us to see the richness and strength of our neighbors and fellow citizens. It can seem easier to serve "the poor" in a country not our own, because we feel that we have no hand in making those people poor; we can explain away our guilt by saying it has nothing to do with us, but is the fault of that country's government, that country's lack of compassion, social mobility, etc. Domestic service trips give us the chance to meet people who are more like us culturally and allow us to look more deeply at issues of injustice here at home. Service trips within our home state or home city can build bridges across the differences which often seem to divide us.

When serving domestically, volunteers encounter marginalized populations and situations about which they already have a narrative. Instead of encountering a person who is experiencing homelessness and reflecting inwardly on why that person is homeless, they already have an answer in mind. That answer could be any number of things—addiction, poor work ethic, uneducated—whatever narrative that the community in which this volunteer grew up has taught them. The gift of serving in one's own country allows volunteers to test those narratives. Volunteers encounter those who live in poverty and share a small part of their life's journey. The people and their stories become real.

Those who are leading a domestic trip assist volunteers to move through the experience with an attitude of openness and learning. These trips require volunteers to move out of their comfort zone, and challenge them to see the reality of the poor in their own country, how they may contribute to injustice, and how they may work to alleviate it. Though this is a complex process, it includes three key aspects to consider—preparation, expectations, and making connections through compassion.

Preparation

Whenever we are taking a trip there is some sort of preparation involved. Basic preparations include finding out how to get there, what to pack, where to stay, and what to do. We prepare because we want things to go smoothly, to know what lies ahead, and to be ready for it. The same is true for a service trip. Each volunteer and leader and the group as a whole must take the time to prepare.

In preparing, it's important for each person to look at their own motivations for signing up for the service trip, to answer the question *Why do I want to serve?* Each person has their own reason for participating, including the noble reasons—to give, to help others, to make a difference. The more you are able to look at your own motivations for wanting to take part in a domestic service trip, the more honest you can be with yourself and those around you, and the more insight you will gain through the experience.

Preparation also includes learning a few things about the place where you will be going. You might want to research the demographics of the area or perhaps some history of how the city or town was founded and developed. For example, you might look up the city's or county's median income, the percentage of high school graduates, and the average age. It might be helpful to know whether the area was settled for a specific reason—perhaps it was chosen by a community seeking religious freedom or by an industry that saw the benefits of the area. This information will help you have a sense of the place where you are going and allow the narrative of this place to begin to take shape. Part of your experience includes comparing what you learned ahead of time with the reality you encounter.

When you begin to learn about where you are going, you inevitably begin to think about your own reality and where you have come from, which is also part of preparing yourself for the experience.

Preparation is not just about learning about the place you will be going; it's also about readying yourself for what you may encounter. As people of faith, prayer is part of the experience. It's important to pray for those you will meet and serve throughout your service trip and to pray that God help each person to be open to receiving the graces that are offered. Prayer readies us for serving and helps us begin to see the world as God sees it.

The preparation you do before the trip will make a great difference in how much you learn and grow throughout the experience. Preparation takes time and commitment, for personal research and reflection as well as for group meetings and discussions prior to the trip.

Expectations

Whether spoken or unspoken, everyone has expectations. Expectations may be subtle, and they may also lead to disappointment if we don't take time to reflect on them. In being a part of a service trip, you might want to change the world or to make a real difference in someone's life. Those are pretty big expectations! One way to manage expectations is to hope—hope that your presence does make a difference to another person; hope that you can and will contribute meaningfully to the communities where you will be. As St. Paul reminds us, "Hope does not disappoint" (Rom 5:5).

It's natural to imagine what will happen during your service trip, especially if you've participated before or heard the stories of other service trips. You might go with an idea of the type of work that you will do or what the people will be like, but there is no guarantee that you'll paint rooms, tutor children, work in a community garden, or serve at a soup kitchen. You may not meet people who are eager to have help or who want assistance. Try to be open and to allow all your experiences to teach you, even any disappointments and challenges you might encounter.

Here at the DePaul Center, we hosted a group of volunteers who returned from a local food warehouse disappointed that they were asked to put boxes together, hundreds of boxes that were to be used in the coming week to make food baskets. They had wanted to do something that felt better, something that seemed to help someone more. We had to remind them that they did what the agency needed and that putting together boxes was indeed service. Sometimes, our expectations of how we want to serve and the needs of the community work sites can be far apart. This experience called the volunteers to reflect—am I here to do what is needed, or do I put limits on what I consider service?

Every experience you have has the capacity to teach you and change you if you take it to heart. It is important to take a step back to reflect on all the experiences that you have during your time of service. Remember, no two trips are the same, so try to be open to what comes your way, especially those moments that may seem disappointing or when you struggle to find meaning in your service.

The following questions can help you to think more about your expectations:

- What does service mean to you?
- What does it mean to do something "for" another versus doing something "with" them?
- Can simply sitting near a child or an elderly person be service?
- Do I consider my presence to another a service?
- Am I serving if I am simply learning?
- Are there limits to what I will or will not do?

Reflecting on expectations can allow you to find clarity in your purpose and can also help you be more open to the many unexpected events that you will experience on your trip.

Connections Made From Reflection

As hosts and guides for domestic volunteers, we feel we have not done a good job if groups leave us the same as they arrived. For us, assisting volunteers to see beyond their experience of service is crucial. Service is a means through which we might look at the bigger issues of social justice and poverty.

If the primary goal of a service trip is to grow, learn, and deepen one's faith, then emphasis must be put on processing and reflecting on the experience. We encourage you to not be content with surface questions and surface answers. We challenge you to go deeper, in order to make lasting connections between your short term service experience and the rest of your life.

To be open to reflection that challenges you to make changes in yourself or your lifestyle, your approach must be rooted in authentic compassion.

Father Greg Boyle, a Jesuit priest who works with current and former gang members, writes that "Compassion isn't just about feeling the pain of others; it's about bringing them in toward yourself. If we love what God loves, then, in compassion, margins get erased. 'Be compassionate as God is compassionate,' means the dismantling of barriers that exclude."

This idea of a transforming compassion is much different than the "compassion" many of us practice. It asks more of us than to just be kind to those we see every day. It requires us to look deeply at every aspect of our lives, in the context of the love and compassion God has offered us, and the call for us to do the same for our brothers and sisters.

A group that approaches their trip with authentic compassion looks very different from a group who does not. We've discovered there are four levels to authentic compassion:

1. It is natural for a person, especially a young person, to feel pride and joy after serving or being with the poor. There is an authentic desire to serve and give of ourselves, and we feel accomplished when we do this. If your reflection after serving 400 people dinner is that you felt proud, or were brought joy by giving to others, this is the beginning stage of compassion. At this stage you have recognized that you can help to alleviate the suffering of others in some small way.

2. If transformation and compassion are the task at hand, group members must challenge one another to "go deeper," beyond the first stage. The next level of authentic compassion would be to recognize how many people needed dinner that night, or in other words, how many people in the immediate area of that soup kitchen were experiencing hunger and food insecurity. This opens you to the larger reality of the situation, perhaps to feelings of sadness or anger, and to the recognition that you are merely providing alleviation of the problem for one night.

3. In reflecting further, you might allow this experience to invite you to live life differently, by challenging you to be more careful not to waste food or to be more compassionate to people experiencing homelessness. Deepening in authentic compassion impacts your personal life and the way you treat others.

4. A group that continues to go deeper would not only recognize the number of people who are going hungry, but would also ask the question "why are so many people going hungry in our country?" This is a harder level to enter because it not only forces you to face the pain of those experiencing hunger, but also the way that each of us contributes to the problem. Asking this question requires looking at your values, our history, and our policies as a neighborhood, city, or country. This depth of reflection and compassion asks you to not only make a change in your personal life, but to look critically at your community's culture and to change what perpetuates and creates this system where so many go hungry.

Living a life of authentic compassion seeks to break down the barriers that exclude, where we go beyond platitudes and prayers for those who suffer. Getting to this level of compassion is not easy. Passionate and compassionate guidance helps us to feel more comfortable asking the challenging and painful questions that will lead to a deeper compassion—a compassion that demands more than service; it demands action and change.

Conclusion

Domestic service trips are a chance to meditate on intentions, to test stereotypes, and to build bridges of compassion through encounter. Through preparation, managing expectations, and building authentic compassion through reflection, we hope to offer volunteers an opportunity to allow their time in mission to create a ripple effect through the rest of their lives. Considering each of these aspects, you will be challenged to see that this world of our faith—compassion, service, encounter, valuing, and standing with the vulnerable—is something very intimately connected to every part of life, and to answer God's call to view the Gospel as an example of what it looks like to live a radically loving and compassionate life.

Darcy O'Hara is a graduate of Mount Saint Mary's University and has been both a volunteer and leader on a number of domestic service trips with Mt. St. Mary's Office of Social Justice. Sr. Sharon Horace is a Daughter of Charity who has ministered among various cultures, both internationally and domestically for 20 years. Darcy and Sr. Sharon have coordinated and facilitated service retreats for volunteers from over 50 high school and college groups at St. Vincent DePaul Young Adult Center in Germantown, PA.

What's Appropriate?

by Julie Lupien

When we move out of our comfort zones and travel to someone's home or neighborhood, we automatically become a guest. Being invited is an honor. As guests we are no longer in charge. Our hosts guide us in ways to behave that show respect and will keep us safe.

Mission experiences take us to places that are very different from what we are used to. We will be noticed! Everything we say, do, and wear sends a message that will be interpreted through *their* cultural lens, *not* ours. Some may even have certain expectations of us because we are Christians. For this reason it is very important to have someone who understands the culture to advise us on what is appropriate. We may be invited to dress or act differently than at home. We always keep in mind, this is their home and we are the guests.

Each culture has different rules about appropriate dress. Our society has become much more casual in how we dress. The issue is not, what do *they* wear there, but how do we dress that demonstrates how special this experience is for us? Clothing that *may* not be appropriate in some cultures or situations includes: shorts, sleeveless tops, pants for women, or short skirts.

Our dress is the first thing others will see; how we behave sends even more messages. Respectful behavior is different in each culture. Our manners have become more casual in our society, too. Many cultures would view our lack of formality as rude. Areas of sensitivity include how loud our voices are, how we greet people, how elders are addressed and shown respect, or the way we joke, since it can easily be misunderstood.

There are two issues that require special attention—male-female interaction and drinking. For cultural and safety reasons, it would be wise that participants be with at least one other group member whenever possible, and never alone with someone of the opposite sex as it might be perceived as inappropriate. In many cultures, couples do not show affection in public, so any couples within the group should respect this during their experience. Group members might want to avoid drinking alcohol during the experience. It may seem like the sociable thing to do and it may be how we relax at home; however, depending on where you serve, it may send a message that could contradict all the other positive things the group does.

Last and certainly most important is safety. Our world, including our own country, struggles with violence. Witnessing the violence of poverty and injustice that exists where we go is hard enough; it would be tragic for something to happen to one of the participants during this experience. Unfortunately, in some instances, participants have been assaulted or robbed. Nowhere in the world is completely safe. But, most places are safe enough for us to visit if, and only if, we listen to our leaders and local guides. In our own communities, there are places and situations we avoid because of safety concerns. The same is true where we visit. Even though things may appear to be safe, there may be situations that we as guests are not aware of. Only our guides can determine where we go, when, and with whom. This is not a joke. Not listening to those in charge can damage much more than just the experience.

Following the advice of our guides about what is appropriate will help us to connect with those we go to accompany ... which is our reason for going in the first place.

Julie Lupien serves as Executive Director of **From Mission to Mission.**

Mission in Reverse: A Volunteer Discovers Ministry as a Conversion Experience

by Michelle A. Scheidt, DMin

> *It is not about knowing; it's about seeking.*
>
> *It is not about having; it's about creating.*
>
> *It is not about a final result;*
>
> *It's about the small outcomes that occur along the way.*

Jane wrote this reflection while volunteering in an inner city Chicago neighborhood. Her reflections show that she learned to approach her ministry not just as volunteer work but as a missionary and from the perspective of mission in reverse.

Mission means going beyond our boundaries—being challenged, being converted, not necessarily feeling at home all the time. In *Bread for the Journey*, anthropologist Anthony Gittins states: "Unless we seek the margins and the people who live there, a dimension of our Christian lives will remain unexplored and a whole vista of mission will remain unseen, out of sight. The wonderful thing is that the vista is visible almost from where we are; just a short, committed, faith-filled step across our margins is all that is required." Jane made that step by coming to Chicago from an upper middle-class family on Long Island, ready to live out her deep faith and help people in need. She admits that she came with great enthusiasm, some fears, and some idealism as well: "I wanted to give something back to the world, to help in some way," she said. "I wanted to be doing work that was needed, making a difference in someone's life."

Many volunteers arrive with faith-filled and altruistic motives like Jane's only to find that, instead of changing lives, they are changed themselves. Volunteers confront urban challenges such as poverty, violence, gangs, and other facts of urban life which are systemic realities that cannot be changed overnight. With consistent efforts over many years, some positive changes emerge; however, what are truly being transformed are short-term volunteers and their beliefs about ministry, poverty, people, and who they are called to be in the world. Jane said, "I do notice that there has definitely been a change in me; I pray for that all the time. I know that that's happening, but it's not because of what I decided." Jane experienced mission in reverse.

Mission in reverse refers to a way of approaching ministry, an attitude which is an essential component of being a missionary. The mission in reverse approach means that we as ministers allow ourselves to grow, change, and learn from people who are different from us. If we minister from the perspective of mission in reverse, we enter a situation with open hands and open hearts; we seek not to lead or control or bring truth but to be led and taught and converted by people who are marginalized.

In many ways, the mission in reverse approach is completely opposite of the traditional concept of being a missionary; the idea contradicts many people's reasons for becoming a minister in the first place. We may decide to volunteer because we think we have something great to give and want to share our knowledge and resources with people who we think have less than we do. In the process of trying to give, we discover that rather than helping others we are growing and learning ourselves. We experience conversion. Claude Marie Barbour describes it in *Seeking Justice and Shalom in the City*:

> The mission-in-reverse approach teaches that the minister can and should learn from the people ministered to—including, and perhaps especially, from the poor and marginal people. By taking these people seriously, by listening to them and indeed learning from them, personal relationships are developed, and the dignity of people is enhanced. Such presence to people is seen as necessarily allowing them to be the leaders in the relationship ... What the minister desires to achieve by his/her total presence to the people is to enable them to see alternatives and to choose to remove the stumbling blocks that prevent them from becoming fully human persons. The same process of being enabled to remove stumbling blocks to personal growth is also relevant for the minister, so that there is a true mutuality in which the minister is ministered unto.

Mission in reverse is what short-term mission is really about. By the time volunteers get to know the people around them and what they are supposed to do, the experience is over—and they might feel that they never really did much "work." Volunteering with the attitude of mission in reverse removes the emphasis on doing and places the value on presence. Getting to know and forming relationships with the people then becomes the primary task. If volunteers are truly going to be open to learning from the people, what they actually "accomplish" or "get done" is of little importance. The biggest thing that happens during the experience is their own growth and change.

Of course, our conversion does not come without cost. We are called to go outside our comfort zones, to let go of our desire to be the one who possesses the truth, to give up the need to control. We must make ourselves vulnerable. The process is scary and we have to surrender to uncertainty, but most ministers discover that they receive far more than they give.

"Maybe I'm not making a difference at all," Jane said. In embodying the spirit of mission in reverse, she discovered that the experience impacted her whole life: "Volunteering goes everywhere with you; you never get rid of it." Volunteering helped Jane begin developing her own missionary vocation with service as a way of life.

Jane ends her poem with powerful words that describe her journey:

> *It's complete contentment with the moment and complete faith in the future. It is all I have ever wanted and I found it amidst the tagging, the prostitution, the gang warfare, the poverty, the sick, the dying, the dead, the depressed, the suicidal, the discouraged, the children, the adolescents, the alcohol, the drugs, the misunderstandings, the sleep deprivation, the injustice, the lies, the hungry, the homeless, the violence, the gunshots, the fires, the pain, the tears ....*

A young woman of twenty-two discovered complete contentment and all she ever wanted by volunteering in the inner city. She experienced mission in reverse.

Michelle A. Scheidt has worked in the nonprofit sector for 25 years and is currently a program officer at the Fetzer Institute, which is dedicated to helping build the spiritual foundation for a loving world. She served as a lay volunteer for two years and later co-directed the Claretian Volunteer and Lay Missionary Program in Chicago. Michelle has extensive intercultural experience in inner city Chicago and in Latin America. She holds a Master Arts in Pastoral Studies from Catholic Theological Union and a Doctor of Ministry from Chicago Theological Seminary.

The Invitation to Mission—"Come And See"

by Matt Rousso

There is a memorable scene recorded in the Gospel of John (1:38–39) about the day two disciples were caught following Jesus. When Jesus realized they were following him, he turned asking them, "What do you want?" They replied, "Rabbi, where do you live?" And he replied, "Come and see!"

This is precisely the invitation extended to us when are called into a short-term mission program—to leave one's home in order to go and see how other people are living. There is a mission program in Mexico that even calls itself the "Come and See" program. When I first began to work as a Maryknoll Mission Educator, I was told that mission education is about "helping others to know the reality of Third World peoples—their sufferings and sorrows as well as their hopes and joys." What I have come to learn as I have engaged in this ministry of mission education over the past fifteen years is that seeing is much more than what meets the eye. When Jesus explained to some of his disciples why he spoke in parables, he answered "because these people's hearts have grown dull; they have ears but can barely hear, eyes but they do not see" (Mt 13:15).

I believe these words of Jesus challenge all of us who engage in missionary work to look deeply into the reality we encounter. Reality is like an onion—it has many layers. When we first look at the situation of people to whom we go, we see people living in abject poverty, in conditions that cry out for relief—from hunger, from inadequate health and dental care, from crude housing. And because we are compassionate people, we feel great pity. Only a year ago I was walking with a group of missionaries through an extremely poor neighborhood called Soyopango, near the city of San Salvador. I began to get a whiff of a very foul odor and as we turned the corner, we were confronted with a large garbage dump—people were rooting around, looking for vegetables that might be edible or other useful things. It was a very pitiful sight!

That day in El Salvador, I realized again that as a mission educator my work is not simply to bring others on mission programs so they can see people suffering and feel sorry for them. That is only the first step—the top layer of the reality. Good mission education must enable people to look more deeply— to see the outer layer of reality and ask, "What's beneath this?" What is going on that creates such a reality or sustains such a reality? That kind of questioning is sometimes referred to as *social analysis*— which can be really challenging because it brings us to the point where we have to look at things we'd rather not see.

Today we are beginning to understand much more clearly that the reality of Third World peoples is very often influenced by and indeed, in many instances, actually created by the foreign policies of the G8 nations (which includes our own United States) and the World Bank—policies regarding issues like free trade, money borrowing, patent rights, and the sales and distribution of military armaments, etc. We are dumbfounded by actions of suicide bombers and rebellious militants. Why do they do such atrocious acts, often against their own people? In his 1999 Peace Day Message, Pope John Paul II offered an answer to that rhetorical question: "When human rights are ignored or scorned, and when the pursuit of individual interests unjustly prevails over the common good, then the seeds of instability, rebellion and violence are inevitably sown." If we dare to ask depth questions, we must be open to finding answers that may unsettle us.

Our mission trips to Mexico or Guatemala or Thailand or wherever should lead us to ask depth questions; to want to know the causes of suffering, of poverty, of oppression. As mission theologian David Bosch says, "The practice of mission is enhanced greatly by an ongoing study of mission and by social analysis." There are so many good resources and people who can readily help us to look at what lies more deeply beneath the surface—beginning with our religious leaders, especially those who live and minister in Third World countries. When the United States Congress was preparing to vote on a Free Trade Policy for several Latin American countries, Bishop Alvaro Ramazzini, President of the Bishops' Secretariat of Central America and Panama, strongly opposed its passage saying, "Our analysis of the official CAFTA texts confirms the enormous dangers its implementation will pose, potentially affecting our rights, our environment, our well-being. CAFTA is based on a logic that favors profit over human rights and sustainability." Unfortunately his words were not heeded and CAFTA passed. When he looks beneath the garbage in the dumps in places like Guatemala, El Salvador, or Honduras, he sees CAFTA!

Albert Nolan, the noted South African missionary, says that our service to the poor must develop; we must go on a journey of conversion. The journey begins, says Nolan, with simple *compassion*—I see the sufferings of others and feel compassion; I want to do something to help, to give them something, to say something that will soothe, to reach out a caring hand. And, if we allow ourselves to look more deeply, we will discover that poverty is a structural problem—the direct result of political and economic structures. This discovery may bring us to indignation or anger, and to wanting to do something more lasting; it is this kind of awareness that even makes us want to find a way to change the world by *promoting structural change*. A deeper conversion will bring us to great *humility* as we face the sufferings of the peoples of the world. In time, we will finally be led to a commitment of true and *deep solidarity*.

Like the two disciples who followed Jesus long ago, we have asked, "Where do you stay?" And we have heard Jesus say, "Come and see." And each time we go to see, Jesus calls us further and further—to look ever more deeply; to see much more than what meets the naked eye. Our hope is that we will not be like those with calloused hearts and dull vision but that Jesus will be able to exclaim of us as he did of his first disciples, "Blessed are your eyes, for they see; and your ears because they hear" (Mt 13:16).

Matt Rousso is currently Director of the Maryknoll Mission Education Center in New Orleans, LA. Since 1991 Matt has been associated with the Maryknoll Missionaries, directing the Maryknoll Mission Education and Promotion Office in New Orleans. His mission experience includes serving in Ecuador and directing Third World mission experience programs in Central American countries (Nicaragua, Guatemala, Honduras and El Salvador).

We Are in Mission to Mission to Mission to Mission to ...

by Christine Garcia, SSND

Celebrate, you are in mission! We are in mission! Celebrate! Do not be afraid! You are loved by God, called, chosen, and claimed by Christ and the Church for a life in mission! You and I, we've been "signed-up" since baptism! Celebrate! Take heart! You have been launched, have been put in motion and you won't ever stop ...

"What's been my mission, my vocation?" you ask? No matter whether at home, sent for a number of years, months, weeks, or days to another land, the mission has been, is still the same: to tell the world with your life that you know that God's love is for all people. We are loved, called, and sent to proclaim that the Realm of God is here. The ultimate mission we have is to live and promote life in such a way that people will believe that they and all people share in the oneness of God in the Trinity. Each moment lived in awareness that we are in mission allows God to continue to transform us for the transformation of the world.

As you move forward in response to a short or long-term commitment in a particular place, with a particular people, allow God's Spirit to work in and through you. Be attentive to that transforming Spirit longing to fill you and that is already in you and those you will meet and will serve. May peace be yours in realizing that you, that each of us, are only a small part of God's larger plan for the transformation of the world. Likewise, if we each stay out of the picture, the picture will be unfinished. Let us offer our lives and trust God's hand in placing us wherever and for whatever length of time God wants in order to make the picture complete.

Also realize that mission is a lifestyle, a way of life. For that reason, when an experience (whether it is short-term or long-term) is over, it really does not end. We continue to be transformed by the experience. And that transformation, when we let the Sprit move in us, leads us to work for justice and peace, to social action, to another short or long-term experience. It may even lead us to a new commitment such as religious life or priesthood. That is why we can say that the experience is never over. Because we are enflamed with the Spirit, we live what we have learned, we continue in mission in new ways, new places, with new people.

The energy that imbued, that enflamed, which launched the early church into mission, is that same fire that ignites you. Like the apostles who couldn't be contained or content to stay behind the safety of the locked doors, take courage and remember you do not, will not walk alone. And if you find yourself dallying behind the doors of uncertainty or disbelief, remember Jesus came through them, anyway. So, take heart. Jesus the Lord who called you, claimed you, has never left you and never will. "Go ... I am with you always, until the end of the age" (Mt 28:20).

Christine Garcia, SSND, serves on the Leadership Council for the School Sisters of Notre Dame – Central Pacific Province. Her cross-cultural experience took her to Lahore, Pakistan, for 16 months. Christine and others in her community were not able to remain and serve in Pakistan as hoped because of the events of 9/11/01.

CHAPTER 3:
Practicalities for Leaders

Short-term mission experiences require a great deal of planning, organizing, and the help of the Spirit. Leading a short-term experience is a great responsibility. If you are a leader, we say "thank you!" This commitment, when done well, requires time and sacrifice. We appreciate your willingness. We know that leaders of short-term experiences play a major role in the entire mission experience: before, during, and after. This section of the guide is for you.

Each mission experience is different. Each group is different. Each way of approaching the mission experience is different. This section looks at the practicalities of the short-term experience, including specific details to be implemented during each phase of the Missioning Process, looking at discernment from the leader's perspective, and understanding culture.

What is presented here is included for a reason: It is important for each and every group to consider. However, every group may not have the time, resources, or ability to complete everything suggested here. Ideally, each group would follow the suggestions provided and more. You must determine how to address each aspect in a way that fits your situation. The important thing to remember is that we dishonor the people we go to be with if we do not prepare to meet them. It is also an injustice to expose our participants to poverty, suffering, and cultural differences without preparation. Equally important, we need to recognize that devoting time to prayer and reflection before, during, and after the experience influences the impact and integration of the experience for the participants.

Throughout "Practicalities for Leaders" you will find page references to activities in the "Tool Kit for Reflection" that correspond with the topic being explained. Following the outlines for each phase of the experience, you will find extensive explanations for three important aspects of the Missioning Process—Discernment, Crossing Cultures, and Integration.

Preparation Phase

The preparation phase is the period prior to the experience, when everyone involved completes responsibilities that will help make the experience a success. This includes the sending group, each participant, and the receiving group who will lead and coordinate the details at the site where the group will be going. This phase includes the following components:

Communication With Sending and Receiving Group Leaders

A major factor in the planning process of a mission experience is communication between the sending group and the receiving group. Communication can make or break the experience. The following are ways that sending group and receiving group leaders contribute to successful mission experiences:

- clearly state and understand expectations;
- plan thoroughly and collaboratively;
- define and agree upon roles and responsibilities;
- complete assigned responsibilities as agreed;
- make decisions with collaboration and respect while honoring your purpose;
- identify a "bridge" person(s) with knowledge of both cultures to assist with orientations on both sides;
- communicate clearly, with appropriate detail and timeliness.

Discernment and Selection

Encourage all those interested in participating in the mission experience to go through a period of discernment before completing the application process. Everyone involved in the mission experience has his or her own questions on which to focus (see pages 61-65, 74-76).

The individual missioner gathers information about the experience and discusses it thoroughly with a discernment partner. The main questions are:

- What is my motivation for wanting to do this?
- What is my motivation for wanting to be part of this group?
- Do I have the qualities and maturity to do this with this group?
- Am I ready to participate in this mission experience?

The sending group leaders go through a period of assessment and discernment concerning each potential group member and answer the following questions:

- Is this person ready for this type of experience at this time?

- Is this person right for the group?

- Is this person right for the people and culture where we are going?

The receiving group gathers information about the group and carefully looks at the following:

- Who are the missioners and from where do they come?

- What do they offer us?

- What do we need from this group?

- How do we prepare them to understand the culture enough to enter into it?

- What do we need to do to prepare for their arrival?

Practical Issues

Short-term mission experiences require signficant planning and organizing well in advance of the group being formed. Many questions need to be answered, including:

- Do the church leadership and community support this mission experience?

- What are the goals for this experience?

- What are the criteria for deciding where to go and when?

- Will we organize our own mission experience or link with an organization?

- What are the expectations of this organization?

- Who is the contact person?

- How will we travel? Where will we stay? How will meals be handled?

- How much will this cost? Who will finance it? How will we raise the funds?

- What special expenses will this require, such as insurance?

- What are the maximum and minimum number that can participate?

- Are we being invited to participate in a service project?

- What skills and numbers are needed for the project?

- What are our timeline and specific tasks to make this mission experience a reality?

Once the preliminary work has been completed, it is time to get the community involved and form the group that will participate. This includes:

- advertising the details of the mission experience and hosting an information session;

- engaging those interested in the discernment process;

- initiating the application process;

- educating the larger community about this mission experience; and

- inviting the community to participate in and support the experience.

Leadership is important. Developing group leaders includes:

- discerning of group leaders;
- identifying leadership roles, responsibilities, and communication;
- committing to specific responsibilities; and
- planning ways to support the leadership team.

When the group is formed, many details need to be addressed:

- expectations of the group before, during, and after the experience;
- lines of communication between the leaders and the group;
- meeting schedule;
- travel details to, from, and during the mission experience;
- daily schedule while on site;
- expectations for each day, including prayer, processing, service, and rest;
- health issues and vaccinations for the area to which you will be traveling;
- packing list;
- supplies that may need to be brought for the project; and
- plan for the group upon return.

Community Building

There is a big difference between a group of individuals and a community. Becoming a Christian community does not just happen because the members are Christian or because we all know each other. When short-term mission groups become a community, we demonstrate the presence of Jesus Christ that combines all of our personalities and gifts. Devoting time to building a sense of community within the group and getting to know each other will have a major impact on the entire experience. Together we practice what will happen during the experience: being open, being present, sharing faith, and offering compassion in the service of others (see pages 76-85).

We might begin by learning about each individual's

- faith journey;
- motivation for participating;
- hopes, expectations, and fears;
- history of crossing cultures; and
- strengths, weaknesses, skills, and what they have to offer this experience.

Next we build a sense of community by

- articulating the importance of building community within the group;
- using prayer, reflection, journaling, and processing that will be done throughout each phase of the experience;
- practicing relationship skills: cooperation, mutual respect, listening, understanding another's view, flexibility, adaptability, and conflict resolution;

- getting to know the personality differences and the learning and communication styles of each member of the group; and

- utilizing team-building games and activities.

Agree on how the group will operate by

- establishing lines of communication within the group;

- creating a covenant within the group for the entire experience;

- coming to consensus on the style and process of group decision-making and conflict resolution;

- determining expectations and committing to group activities before, during, and after the experience; and

- creating a code of behavior to be used throughout the experience (see pages 39 and 76).

Understanding Mission

Each member of the group may have a different motivation for being part of this experience, as well as a different understanding of mission. An important step in becoming a community is creating a unified understanding of what *our* purpose is for this mission experience. We begin by learning about what others have said about mission (see pages 9-13, 21-44, 96):

- What does scripture tell us about mission?

- What does our church tell us about mission?

Then we develop our own understanding of our mission purpose and live it by

- discussing evangelization and the other components of mission found in "What is Mission?" on pages 9-13;

- exploring the concepts of openness, presence, transformation and solidarity from "What is Mission?" on pages 12-13 and 78;

- discussing the values of giving and receiving, mutuality, hospitality;

- creating a group mission statement or theology of mission;

- practicing mission *here*, not just *there*; and

- choosing a theme for the experience using scripture or other meaningful quotes.

Understanding How to Approach Another Culture

The focus of the mission experience is the people we go to accompany. We go to be with others we would never meet at home. When learning about the people and their culture is a priority, it helps us to offer our best to those we meet and to treat them with honor and respect. We begin with learning about culture including (see pages 66-69, 81-82):

- understanding what culture is;

- looking at the cultural background of each group member;

- discussing where our borders and boundaries are;

- exploring feelings about moving out of our comfort zone;

- learning the guidelines for approaching another culture;

- using cross-cultural exercises or simulation games.

We learn ways of dealing with culture shock as suggested by L. Robert Kohls in *Survival Kit for Overseas Living: For Americans Planning to Live and Work Abroad*.

- The best remedy to culture shock is to know as much as possible about where you are. Ask questions; use all your resources to learn as much as you can about the location and people.

- Look for logical reasons behind everything which seems strange. This will be a positive reinforcement that there is a logical explanation behind everything.

- Resist the temptation to disparage the host culture, and do not hang around others who do—they only want to get you on their side.

- Talk about some of your problems with a host national with whom you feel comfortable.

- Have faith—in yourself, the host country/culture/people, and in the positive outcome of the experience.

We look at the specifics of the culture to which we are going, by

- exploring the culture, history, geography, economic situation, etc. of this culture;

- looking at the norms for females and males in this culture;

- learning about communication in this culture;

- discussing gift-giving and using money;

- learning the important moral issues for this culture and how to respect them;

- practicing critical observation and social analysis for our own country before applying it to another; and

- learning basic language skills.

Commissioning

We are sent by God and by our community. A ritual of sending forth by our faith communities, families, and friends can be an important part of the mission experience and also helps us to remember that God is the one who sends us, that we represent more than ourselves, and that we have a responsibility to bring back what we learn for the good of those who send us (see page 85).

Insertion Phase

The insertion phase is a time of ongoing engagement with the culture and life of the people we go to accompany. It is the cross-cultural experience itself. The effectiveness of this stage will depend a great deal on how we have handled the tasks of the preparation phase. This phase includes orientation, evaluation, and daily processing, with a number of key components to consider:

Cultural and Language Orientation

The receiving group who will act as guides during this experience provide important information, including the basic language skills and cultural background that will help the group to enter into this culture. It is critical to have a guide who understands the local reality, who can "translate" not just the language, but also the culture. This includes

- information about the people with whom we will be working;
- history of the country, area, and church;
- current social, economic, and political reality;
- any specific sensitivities, things not to do;
- ways to show respect;
- norms of hospitality;
- gift-giving;
- photo etiquette; and
- language learning, including greetings and important phrases.

Provide specific information for the group including:

- expectations of each individual as well as the group;
- rules, boundaries, schedules;
- safety issues;
- appropriate behavior;
- common sense behavior;
- appropriate clothing;
- health issues, precautions;
- food issues;
- handling emergencies;
- contact people; and
- what behavior will result in being sent home.

Daily Prayer, Reflection, and Processing

Each day the community comes together to pray, support, and help each other understand what is being witnessed and experienced. This time of processing has a major influence on finding the meaning of the experience and later integrating what is learned. Daily prayer and processing of the experience are essential; if it is not logistically possible for the group to gather, this processing may be done individually. Leaders are strongly encouraged to make daily participation a requirement for every group member. There are many ways to structure this time, such as those suggested here and other examples on pages 86–88.

- begin each day with brief prayer and a thought or question for the day;

- conclude each day with prayer, processing, and journaling;

- journal about anything significant so that it can be reviewed later;

- use a scripture reading, quote, or theme throughout (the same one, or change daily);

- include mission theology and church teaching; and

- rotate the leader for group processing.

As the group learned during the community building activities of the preparation phase, everyone is different and each will deal with what happens during this mission experience differently. It is important to remember to:

- provide time and space for those who need quiet time to process, as well as for those who need to talk it out;

- deal with things as a community whenever something happens that effects someone in the group, even though all may view what happened differently;

- have a leader available for anyone who needs more time processing; and

- deal with any major events that impact the group, including news from home, world events, or something happening in the place where you are.

Continued Cultural Understanding

As the group moves through the experience, it is essential to have someone from the receiving group or a cultural guide to provide ongoing education about the local culture. This time of processing allows for discussion about the culture based on that day's activities. Cultural guides might include:

- the receiving group;

- a local leader who helps to interpret the experience;

- returning volunteers who have experienced this culture previously; or

- other local people who may be invited to the group's sharing time, as appropriate given any language or other limitations.

Processing time is devoted to dealing with the feelings and emotions that arise from encountering the local culture. Culture shock has been defined as the "realization of how inadequately your world fits with their world .... The differences are so strong that they overwhelm our normal coping mechanisms .... Culture shock is the stunning emotions that accompany our move into a different world, usually (but not always) negative" (Leeann Stiles, *Mack and Leeann's Guide to Short-term Missions*). (Refer to page 68 for ways of dealing with culture shock.) Each member of the group focuses on the following questions:

- What have you noticed?
- What is your reaction to what you are seeing?
- How do you feel about it?
- What are you struggling with?
- What does this teach you about your own culture?
- What does this teach you about yourself, God, your country, your church?
- What might God be saying to you through this?

Social Analysis

The root causes of poverty and injustice are looked at in order to promote a deeper understanding of the reality of the lives of the poor. Processing time is needed to understand how these realities came to be, what systems have contributed to this reality, and what feelings surface for us as we learn more. Again, it is critical to have the receiving group or other guides help the group understand these complex issues and how they relate to the local people. A good deal of this processing will continue after the experience is over. Techniques to assist with social analysis include (see pages 83-85, 87-88):

- *But Why? Method* (page 88);
- describe what you see, using all of your senses;
- describe your reactions and feelings using "I" statements;
- make connections to previous life experience and lessons;
- seek information that will help you understand better;
- when approaching local people say "Help me to understand," which demonstrates openness and not judgment;
- ask yourself, "How does this impact my perspective?" Remember that a new perspective does not change the injustice or your feelings, just your understanding;
- ask yourself, "How am I connected to this?"; and
- ask yourself, "What might God be saying to me through this?"

Group Care

Throughout the experience, the group continues to get to know each other and develop as a community. Even though the group shares this experience, each member of the group will go through it differently. Mission experiences can be very challenging. Having the support of the community will be an important part of facing the challenges presented. Factors that contribute to the well being of the group include:

- honoring the group's mission statement, covenant, and agreed upon rules;
- looking out for each other;
- connecting with all members of the group, not just friends;
- paying attention to anything special (birthdays, etc) going on for any individual;
- putting others' needs first;
- being on time and doing what is asked;
- taking care of ourselves;

- speaking our truth in a sensitive, respectful manner;

- keeping each other, especially the leaders, informed about where we are, if we are not feeling well, or anything significant that may have happened;

- being flexible; and

- expecting the unexpected.

Short-term mission experiences are intense. Conflict will happen. Remember to

- practice the conflict resolution techniques developed and agreed to during orientation;

- deal with conflict situations right away;

- provide opportunities for individuals to voice their truth;

- maintain a non-judgmental atmosphere; and

- deal with cliques or romantic relationships that develop by reminding participants that they are part of a group and should not focus on just one or a few within the group.

Personal and Project Evaluation

Evaluation of the entire experience by those involved should take place at various points during the experience, at its end, and after returning home. Quality evaluation done mutually with the receiving group builds up those involved and improves the program (see page 88). Do not forget to

- start by looking at the group mission statement and expectations;

- affirm what was done well that needs to continue;

- sensitively voice what did not go well and what could make it better;

- make sure evaluations are not done when tired;

- continue the evaluation after having more time to reflect on the experience; and

- remember the reason(s) for going.

Closure

Just as the commissioning to go is an important part of the mission experience, so is the way we end our experience in another culture and with our group. Being attentive and intentional with closure has an influence on how well we re-enter our home culture (see pages 88-89).

Saying Goodbye

Saying goodbye to people who matter to us can be difficult and very emotional. Many people avoid it. Making the effort to say goodbye to those who have touched our hearts is one way of honoring them. We acknowledge the goodness of the experience and celebrate the special connection that we will carry in our hearts. It also helps later, when we miss them, to know that we took the time to say goodbye. Consider the following:

- bring meaningful closure to the group and to those with whom the group worked closely, by using prayer, rituals, blessings;

- include local people;

- find ways to thank the local people;

- say goodbye to all significant people, if possible; and

- do not create an expectation of keeping in touch unless you mean to do so.

The group has spent a great deal of time preparing for this experience, and now it is coming to a close. As a group, while still on-site, consider the following:

- acknowledge that the end of this experience includes many endings, such as the end of the experience itself, the end of the group if your group is not going to meet after your return, the completion of a goal, etc.;
- process the feelings that can be identified;
- begin to surface the gifts of the journey;
- pray for the people met there and for that place;
- begin to voice a commitment to what is next; and
- "re-commission" the group for whatever comes next.

Preparing to Re-enter

Anyone who has spent time in another culture and allowed the people and the experience to touch them knows that returning home can be exciting but also difficult. Often participants do not expect the return to be difficult; after all we are returning home. We may be returning to a place we know well, but we may be returning significantly changed by the experience. How do you explain to others this incredible experience and how it has touched you? As leaders we need to prepare our participants for what awaits them.

- If possible, do not return right away. If an extra day or more can be added to the experience— such as for sightseeing—it provides an in-between space where the participants can let what has happened sink in before returning to family and friends.
- Discuss how the group feels about going home and what they expect.
- Prepare the group for what they may find when they return.

Leaders can suggest ways to tell the story that will not overwhelm listeners, including:

- choose highlights (without details) about the group, people you met, things you did;
- prepare different versions of your story: 3 minutes, 10 minutes, and a long version.

Last bits of advice

- Use the companion book to this guide—*Remaining Faithful: A Guide for Reflecting on Short-Term Mission Experiences*—which was created to help with further processing and integration.
- Remind the group of dates when the group will gather at home.
- Emphasize the importance of continued prayer and journaling.
- Encourage all to be patient with themselves and those at home with whom they share.
- Remind the group to get plenty of rest so that they offer their best to their family and friends.
- Encourage the group not to judge others if they do not understand the experience or if they do not agree with any new thoughts or opinions that have come from this experience.
- Remind the participants to continue praying.

Return Phase

The return phase is the time when we prepare to leave the culture we have been visiting, return home, and focus on the work of integration. The return phase is often referred to as the "neglected side of mission" because most groups do nothing when they return. Taking the time to focus on the experience after you return is the difference between "what I did on my summer vacation" and a transformative experience (see pages 70-72, 91-95). Components include telling the story, remembering, integration, healing, and finding ways to continue the journey.

Telling the Story

One of the best ways to honor the experience and to continue to learn from it is to tell our story. Each time we tell our story we look at the experience and what it means to us. Each time, we may discover something new, or we might come to realize what mattered the most. Telling our story is also a way to be a bridge between our home culture and the culture we visited. Storytelling suggestions include:

- think of stories ahead of time;

- write your story;

- tell the story whenever you can, as often as you can;

- paint verbal pictures to help your listeners connect with what you share;

- focus on the people you met, not on statistics;

- accentuate the positive;

- share the reality of what you witnessed from your perspective;

- be honest and do not exaggerate; and

- share important lessons, what impacted you the most, how it has challenged you.

As group leaders we can encourage group members to tell their stories by

- finding ways for group members to share their story, such as making presentations to classes, other service groups in and out of the church; and

- organizing a reunion for members and their families for a night of storytelling and photo sharing.

Sharing With Our Faith Community

We are sent by our communities to represent them wherever we are called. We return to them filled with a greater understanding of God, God's people, and our own call to mission. We also bring back the gifts and skills that were developed or enhanced by this experience, to share as we minister here at home. We have an obligation to share the experience and what we learned with those who sent us. They have an obligation to be open to what we share and to the possibility of being changed by it. Leaders can help this happen by

- organizing a presentation for the community;

- assisting group members with reflection questions and guidance for their sharing;

- encouraging group members to be involved in the faith community by sharing the same skills used as we ministered during this short-term experience; and

- sharing evaluation results with community leadership.

Ongoing Reflection

"Experience is not the best teacher. We learn nothing from experience. We only learn from reflection on the experience" (Tony Saddington). If we want the experience to live on in our lives and not just become a memory, we must take time to look at what the experience meant to us and find ways to integrate what was learned. Consider

- reading *Remaining Faithful: A Guide for Reflecting on Short-Term Mission Experiences*, a resource for ongoing prayer and reflection;
- referencing the *Tool Kit* (pages 73-96) for more information;
- continuing to journal;
- going back to what was written during the experience and spending more time looking at the thoughts and feelings recorded at that time and reacting to them now;
- continuing to meet as a group for some time after the experience to process, similar to what was done before and during the experience;
- continuing to use the prayers, songs, and scripture from the experience;
- reviewing mission theology: openness, presence, transformation, and solidarity;
- creating a system to share information about the situation and people at the service site;
- asking for additional evaluation feedback; and
- gathering for a retreat in 3–6 months, since time will offer different insights.

Healing the Hurts

Short-term mission experiences often include painful aspects. This might include the pain of seeing someone suffer, violence that took place while you were there, learning something difficult, conflict in the group, or even disappointment with the experience itself. It is important to deal with the painful parts in a healthy way so that the hurtful parts are not all we remember.

Participants may find it helpful to

- reflect on what happened;
- acknowledge the lessons learned;
- pray and ritualize the letting go of the negative;
- pray for healing and forgiveness;
- seek help from someone you trust if these feelings continue; and
- move forward in a new way.

Remembering the Gifts of the Journey

Many participants of short-term mission experiences have returned home knowing that we have received far more than we gave. We will never be the same because of the gifts we received from witnessing how others live their lives and their faith. By becoming more aware of the gifts received, we learn to integrate the short-term experience into our daily lives. Reflect on the following questions:

- Who made a positive impact on you and why?
- What have you learned that you hope never to forget?
- How are you different because of this experience?
- What values did you witness that had an impact on you?

- What did the people teach you about yourself?
- What is God saying to you through these memories?

Integration

We integrate the experience and what we learned when we remain faithful to who we have become. We can begin to do this by

- recognizing how we have been changed by this experience, including our attitudes, beliefs, values, skills, behaviors, and what we learned;
- reviewing "Transformation" from "What is Mission?" (page 13) and "Integration" (pages 70-72); and
- using the "What?" model in *Remaining Faithful*, or other methods found in the *Tool Kit* (pages 91-95).

Staying Involved

One way participants of short-term mission experiences integrate the experience is to commit to further involvement at home. Consider the following suggestions:

- define how to live in solidarity with those people met during the experience;
- continue to serve locally, both individually and as a group;
- find organizations that are committed to the issues discussed during your experience;
- pray and fast while being conscious of the needs of others;
- simplify your lifestyle;
- advocate for those issues and people you learned more about during this experience by sharing your story;
- do something about the injustices you learned about and their root causes by writing letters, joining demonstrations, boycotting businesses;
- continue to be educated about peace and justice issues;
- use art, music, and photographs from the culture you experienced to remind you to be faithful to what you learned there;
- connect with the social justice teachings of your church; and
- make conscious choices about how you spend your time and resources.

Finding Others Who Understand

Short-term mission experiences affirm the value of Christian community. We are not alone. Together we can make a difference much greater than individually. We need others to guide us and support us when we make a long-term commitment to peace, justice and service. Consider

- forming a small Christian community with like-minded people;
- looking for organizations, locally and globally, that focus on issues you feel most passionate about and getting involved;
- joining or forming a social concerns or social justice committee at church;
- paying attention to events related to your interests in the community; and
- tapping into church resources for further support or involvement, such as Catholic Relief Services; the Catholic Volunteer Network; diocesan offices for mission, peace and justice, or social concerns.

Practical Matters for Leaders

For leaders of short-term mission experiences, the work does not end when you return. Finishing up any end-of-trip details in a timely manner will have a positive influence on your next mission experience. Details include

- getting rest;
- writing thank you notes to the receiving group and any local people who helped the group as well as the supporters from your home community;
- writing a summary of the experience;
- gathering photos and videos to keep on record or to share;
- recording any practical advice for the next mission experience;
- completing any follow-up commitments;
- paying final expenses and preparing a financial report;
- finalizing the evaluation report;
- informing local media of your return from the experience; and
- starting to plan the next mission experience.

NOTES:

Reflection Questions

Which elements listed here are already part of your program?

_____

_____

_____

_____

_____

_____

_____

Based on your time and resources, which elements are the most difficult to incorporate?

_____

_____

_____

_____

_____

_____

_____

Which elements need more attention?

_____

_____

_____

_____

_____

_____

_____

How will you do so?

_____

_____

_____

_____

_____

_____

_____

What is Discernment?

Choosing to be part of a short-term mission experience is a big decision. This decision will impact the lives of many people: Each member of the group; her or his family, friends, and community; and, most importantly, the people who will receive the group. Each must consider, "Is God calling me to encounter my sisters and brothers in another culture as part of this short-term experience?"

Some short-term mission groups accept anyone who signs up. If we are about God's work, how might we invite God into the process, including the question of who will be in the group? As group leaders, with God's help, we can help individuals understand if this mission experience is right for them at this time. We also have the responsibility to decide whether an individual is right for the group at this time. In order to do this it's important to understand what discernment is and how it works.

Discernment is the process of making a decision with the help of the Holy Spirit, the process of discovering God's will for us and then living it. The root meaning of *discern* is "to separate; to sift out," and that is what a good discernment process does. Discernment helps us to separate our motives, to sift out our desires, to sort out our limitations, temptations, misgivings, and feelings. Ultimately, through this sifting, sorting, and separating we can come to that place where we can say to God with deep peace, **"Yes, I am ready to go. Here I am."**

There are many approaches to discernment and many ways to respond to God's call, including the decision to do mission work in a new cultural setting. As we know, God speaks to us in many ways ... through other people, scripture, prayer, nature, our heart, our gut, music, art, as well as others. We need to be open. We need to listen.

The process of discernment consists of four steps:

Step 1: Self reflection

Step 2: Connecting with God

Step 3: Making the decision

Step 4: Confirming the decision

In order for us to be in touch with ourselves and with God, it is vital to approach discernment prayerfully. We need the time, space, and silence to receive what God is saying to us. We need to use our heads and hearts for good discernment. Heads reflect on the situation by looking for information and weighing the advantages and disadvantages of our options. We screen with our hearts what we discover with our head. Prayer that stays in the head and does not engage our feelings makes discernment difficult. Being in touch with our bodies and emotions is essential, for that is another way for us to learn and understand ourselves and our call.

During discernment it is important to involve others who will partner with us as we walk through the discernment process. We may want to consider the perspective they offer:

- Our friends know us and can challenge us. They can help us reflect on the following questions: Is this a good choice for me? Do you think I am ready for this decision? Do you think I can do this? For young people it is important that they partner with an adult as they discern, and not just friends.

- A spiritual director functions in an objective way and assists by reflecting what is heard and seen in our verbal and nonverbal communication. An effective spiritual director helps us focus our consciousness and offers affirmation, encouragement, and support.

- A counselor has a psychology or social work background to help us understand our psychological and emotional history and make-up, and how that fits with what we are discerning.

- A pastoral minister or campus minister knows our story and can help us understand if this choice is consistent with our faith life.

- The mission group leader will have the broader picture of where we will be going and what we may be dealing with when we get there. They know the personal qualities and skills needed for this experience and can help us decide if this opportunity is a good match for us.

The decision-making process is very practical. The following simple suggestions can be brought to prayer and to our discernment partners:

- identify the possible choices—it is important to have more than one option to choose from;

- make a list of the pros and cons of each option;

- take some quiet time and pray with this list;

- pay attention to the feelings or thoughts that surface about each option;

- assess whether the choice made is consistent with your values;

- ask yourself if this choice brings you peace, joy, or other feelings; and if not, what that might mean;

- take some additional time to pray, asking the Spirit for guidance; and

- make a final decision with which your heart, mind, gut, and spirit are at peace.

Robert Longman, Jr., suggests the following hints may help to confirm that a decision is right for us:

- a chance encounter with just the right person;

- a persistent, growing thought or conviction;

- something from scripture keeps coming to mind;

- something said in conversation that just sticks; and

- an opportunity suddenly opens up.

These hints mean nothing by themselves but may be significant when considered together.

Another method of confirmation comes from Peter Kreeft who says, "When you've made your decision, all God's signs should line up, by a kind of trigonometry. There are at least seven such signs:

1. scripture;

2. church teaching;

3. human reason;

4. the appropriate situation, or circumstances;

5. conscience, our innate sense of right and wrong;

6. our individual bent or desire or instincts; and,

7. prayer.

Test your choice by holding it up before God's face. If one of these seven voices says no, don't do it. If none says no, do it."

Discernment Issues for the Sending Group Leader

Not only does each individual need to discern his or her own involvement in the short-term experience, group leaders need to discern as well. As leaders of short-term mission experiences, it is our responsibility to do what we can to make sure that those who participate are right for the experience at this time. As we look at each participant we must ask: Is this person ready for this type of experience at this time? Is this person good for the group? Is this person right for the people to whom we are going? Let us look more at these questions.

Is this person ready for this type of experience at this time?

- Experiencing people of another culture is certainly exciting. Being part of a group that will be traveling to serve God's people is adventurous, fun, and inspirational. At the same time, experiencing poverty firsthand is shocking for anyone. It is not easy to witness the suffering of others, especially when our life seems easy in comparison. Each person deals with witnessing these hardships differently. It is important that each member of the group exhibit a certain degree of spiritual and emotional maturity. Someone who is not ready for this type of experience may be disruptive to the group or may show disrespect to the local people, which could damage the entire experience. Not having the ability to deal with the difficult parts of the experience could also have a lasting, negative effect on the individual as well.

- Short-term mission experiences are for those who truly feel called to serve through this experience. Some may want to go because their friends are going, or because it sounds fun, or because they are looking for something to fill their vacation time. Those to whom we go deserve that we take seriously why we are going and that we truly want to be with them.

- To go and serve God's people in another culture is an honor and privilege earned through a commitment to living our faith, making sacrifices, and engaging in ongoing service. Short-term mission experiences are special opportunities to reach out. Our faith communities and families send us to offer our best for the sake of others. It is important that we send those with a history of serving others.

As group leaders we have a much better understanding of what each person will be asked to do through this experience. As group leaders we also know that short-term mission experiences are powerful and intense and that they are filled with the unexpected. Knowing what you know, you are in a position to evaluate the readiness of each group member for this experience. Someone may feel called, but this does not mean that it is right for them at this time. The leader needs to evaluate the motivation of each group member and whether they are emotionally and spiritually mature enough for what they will be asked to do. Group leaders know there is too much at stake to include someone who has not taken service seriously or is not ready to meet the poor face-to-face.

Our discernment as the group leader is crucial. Through our own prayer and reflection, we may decide to allow someone about whom we may have questions to participate, or we may encourage them to spend some time in service throughout the year and invite them to come back for the next short-term mission experience.

Is this person good for the group?

- When we are called to be part of a short-term mission experience, we are called to the entire experience—before, during, and after. Mission is about offering the love and care of Jesus Christ. Sometimes we think that our love and care are just for the poor; however, love and care are for everyone—group participants, group leaders, supporters, the on-site organizers, and everyone in between.

- The power of short-term mission experiences comes from the collective faith and energy of the group, interacting with the people we meet. Each member brings something unique to the group, and without each the group would be very different. Jesus says, when two or more are gathered together, I am there. When the group does not come together, it is obvious; the focus becomes the group rather than those who receive us. Conflict and pettiness replace the power of God working through us.

Group leaders are responsible for facilitating the group's development of community. Practicing cooperation, collaboration, and mutuality within the group helps us to live this way with others we may not know well. When an individual disrupts the sense of community, this may be a clue to discern whether or not the person is good for the group.

Is this person right for the people to whom we are going?

- Short-term mission experiences bring us to places and people we would never meet at home. Some we meet live very differently than we do and may even speak another language. Most are living in poverty more extreme than we have ever seen before. Some may be suffering from mental illnesses or other diseases. For whatever reason, God has called us to be with them. To approach someone who is different from us, especially under difficult circumstances, takes maturity and courage. No one knows how anyone will react in situations like this. Jesus showed us how to cross cultures. We are to be open, non-judgmental, sensitive, and respectful as we reach out with love and care.

Group leaders are responsible for preparing the group to move out of their comfort zone to meet and be present to all kinds of people. In the end, there may be a member of the group who is just not ready for this encounter. Again, encouragement may lead to his or her individual development over time in preparation for the next mission experience.

When short-term mission experiences involve quality discernment, God's presence can be felt. We know that God is with us before, during, and after the experience. We trust that God will lead us, especially with the difficult decisions we often have to make as leaders.

See pages 74-76 for individual and sending group leader discernment questions.

Reflection Questions

How has discernment been part of your mission program?

_____

_____

_____

_____

_____

In what ways could you do more to help others discern their involvement?

_____

_____

_____

_____

_____

How do you feel about your own discernment as group leader?

_____

_____

_____

_____

_____

How can discernment help you in your role as group leader?

_____

_____

_____

_____

_____

How could you make discernment a more integral part of the mission program?

_____

_____

_____

_____

_____

Crossing Cultures

One of the greatest gifts of the short-term mission experience is the unique opportunity to see another culture up close. Whether we go to an urban area near our home, to the border, or to another continent, we will experience people who live and view the world very differently from us. Each experience in a new culture helps us to see that the Body of Christ is one body with many faces and accents.

What is Culture?

The Mexican American Cultural Center defines culture as, "the particular way in which a human group interprets life and relates with nature, God, the world and other peoples. Culture is not accidental, but an integral part of human life. Culture is lived and expressed through traditions, relationships, food, music, religion, beliefs, thought patterns, myths and how we act. Culture is all encompassing of our lives. It is not only *how* we are it is *who* we are. It is our history, our ethnicity, how we think about our families, who we include in our families, how we speak and when we speak, how we think about God, how we relate to God and the Mother of God. It is how we relate to each other and how we relate to the stranger. We are born into a culture and learn what is right according to our elders. We are formed by our culture. Where we are we bring our culture. It is a core part of us." More simply, culture is the learned and shared values, beliefs and behaviors of a group of people. Or, as theologian Virgilio Elizondo puts it, "culture is the soul of a people."

If the focus of short-term mission experiences is the people we meet, then learning about their culture is a must.

The Influence of Culture

Culture is a lens through which we view the world. What we observe through this lens is filtered by our own values and beliefs. Our values shape our culture and our culture shapes our values. Our behavior, then, is based on what we believe (whether the belief is true or not). We see what we have been trained to see, and we try to make sense of what we see according to our culture. It is important to always remember that different cultures' values and perceptions can be very unique. There is no right or wrong, just different perspectives.

Understanding the values of a particular culture is a starting place for learning. For example: Is time and efficiency valued or is the focus on being present to others? Is present time valued or is the focus on the future? Is the control of one's environment self-determined or fatalistic? In relationship to others, does the culture value the individual or the group?

Our goal is to move from ethnocentrism to ethnorelativism—or moving from the view of being in a room full of mirrors to being in a room full of doors where we can walk in and out of another culture.

Our Own Culture

Many of us have never thought about our own culture until we have had a cross-cultural experience. One of the gifts of a short-term mission experience is coming to know our own culture differently than we would if we did not have this experience. The challenge of the short-term experience comes from seeing our own culture from another perspective, which may bring up many difficult feelings and questions for us.

Each member of the group comes to this experience with a mix of cultural beliefs. Individually we come with our own cultural heritage from our families; for some this may be a strong influence. We come with the influence of where we have lived within our own country; different values that come from living in a rural area versus an urban or suburban area, New England, the Midwest, West Coast, or the South … which are part of our culture as well. And then, we come with the values and perspective that come with being U.S. Americans.

Just as we go with preconceived ideas about the culture to which we are going, the people we will meet will have preconceived ideas about us. Some may only know about U.S. Americans from the news, movies, and television. Some people may not have a positive opinion of the United States. Short-term mission experiences are about connecting with people and not stereotypes, and helping each other to learn the other's reality.

Orientation to the Culture

Orientation to the culture begins during the preparation phase at home. It continues during the initial on-site orientation and throughout insertion, provided by the receiving group. It focuses on learning about the people and region where we will be going. This includes the history, geography, and politics of the region and how these impact the people, as well as the realities of what we will be experiencing. It also includes an introduction to the customs, traditions, and important values for this culture. The group needs to be informed about appropriate behavior and communication while living in this culture. It is important to get this information from the receiving group since they will be the ones who will help to interpret the culture for the visitors.

What we come to understand about the culture will have a lot to do with the length of time we spend there. Some short-term mission experiences last only long enough to get a glimpse of the culture, while others are long enough that we go through a cultural adjustment. No matter the length of time we are there, each day's experiences give us a chance to build our understanding of the culture. Each person will view those experiences through his/her own cultural lens. It is important to have someone from the local culture or someone who knows that culture well help interpret what we witness. Misinterpretations need to be dealt with, or they may ruin the experience.

Communication and Language Learning

Language is the door to the culture, so it is important to learn and use the local language to the extent possible, even if we will be there just a short time. When short-term missioners use greetings and some words or phrases, it shows a real interest and respect for the people. Even if we get things wrong, most people appreciate the effort. The receiving group can suggest words and phrases that will cover our basic needs.

We need to remember that communication involves nonverbal language as well as verbal. The meaning of nonverbal behavior is determined by culture. This includes voice tone, pitch, volume and speed, gestures, dress, silence, expression, eye contact, distance kept from others in communication, and physical contact that may accompany language. That is a lot to understand. Whether or not we know the local language, we too will be communicating nonverbally. Nonverbal communication can easily be misinterpreted, so it is important to listen, clarify what you think was communicated, and have a sense of humor.

How to Approach Another Culture

There is nothing like the feeling of really connecting with someone from a different culture. The following reminders will help us to connect:

- be yourself;

- realize that every culture has positives and negatives, including our own;

- go with an attitude of openness to the new culture;

- aim for curiosity, not judgment, since curiosity leads to understanding; rather than asking "why?" about what we observe, try saying "help me to understand;"

- be sensitive and listen with all your senses;

- respect and follow the standards of behavior presented by the receiving group since they know the culture;

- let the people be the teachers—learn the culture and language from the people's perspective, and let them learn from you too;

- imagine what it would be like to "walk in their shoes;"

- remember the purpose in going: God did not call us to criticize and judge but to view this experience and everyone we meet with the eyes of faith;

- "The world in which you were born is just one model of reality. Other cultures are not failed attempts at being you. They are unique manifestations of the human spirit" (Wade Davis); and

- "Our first task in approaching another people, another culture, another religion, is to take off our shoes, for the place is holy. Else we find ourselves treading on people's dreams. More serious still, we may forget that God was there before our arrival" (John Taylor, *The Primal Vision*).

Reflection Questions

How is cultural understanding and training part of your mission program?

_____

_____

_____

_____

_____

_____

Who will be your guides to understanding the history and culture of the people you will meet?

_____

_____

_____

_____

_____

_____

_____

How will you help the group approach the culture you will visit with sensitivity and respect?

_____

_____

_____

_____

_____

_____

_____

How can you practice communicating with those who speak another language?

_____

_____

_____

_____

_____

_____

_____

_____

Since the focus of any mission experience is the people you go to be with, what more can you do to learn about the people and region you will visit?

_____

_____

_____

_____

_____

_____

_____

_____

_____

Integration: Living the Mission Experience at Home

Your experience is over. You return to tell stories about the people you met and the things you did. For some, once you stop telling the stories this experience will become a very special memory. For others, it might become a stepping stone to further involvement. Upon return, participants of short-term mission experiences often express, "I'll never be the same." Many people do not know what to do with such a powerful experience or how to begin to unpack the lessons learned. These people say, "I feel like my experience is in a box in the closet next to my pictures."

Integration is exploring what you mean when you say "you are not the same," becoming aware of how the experience has impacted you, and finding ways to remain faithful to the learning and values you witnessed. But, integration doesn't just happen—it takes work! With prayer, reflection, and intentionality, your experience can have a lasting impact on your life. Integration is a process that includes several essential elements:

1. **Engage in Reflection**

   Reflecting on the experience and telling stories is more than just reliving it. Reflection helps us to see who and what was most important to us and what continues to challenge us. It helps us to see how we might see things differently.

2. **Identify What Is Important**

   Mission experiences provide opportunities for great learning not just about the people you visited but also about yourself, God, the world, and so much more. Your reflection will help you to recognize what you learned from the people and the values you experienced in the culture. In this stage you identify the learning and values you want to incorporate into your life in a new way, or name how you want to live differently because of your experience.

3. **Make Choices That Honor the Learning and Values You Want to Live**

   Integration does not happen only by identifying what you learned and how you would like to live differently. Integration requires intentional action. It becomes part of us when we find ways to live the values and learning we identified. For example, if you decide you want to live more simply, you need to define what simplicity means to you and what areas of your life you want to change. You define what your actions mean and how it helps you stay connected to your mission experience.

   For questions that will help you go through this reflection process, see pages 91-95 in this guide and the companion book, *Remaining Faithful: A Guide for Reflecting on Short-Term Mission Experiences*.

One of the reasons people say that they feel like their experience is in a box in the closet is that they don't understand how to bring what they learned into their lives. The following are examples of how you might integrate your mission experience.

- **Perspective and Understanding:** You have had your eyes opened to another reality and way of looking at things. Continue to bring a different perspective and understanding of the world and what is important to your current reality and relationships.

- **Be a Bridge Builder:** You have moved out of your comfort zone through this experience to encounter people who are different than you. For a brief period of time you had a foot in two worlds. Continue to find opportunities in your own community to be a bridge between people, especially in reaching out to those on the margins.

- **Practice Social Analysis and Critical Thinking:** Cross-cultural mission experiences teach us to look beneath the surface for meaning and understanding. We learn to look for what contributes to things like poverty and injustice. Continue to look deeper at the issues in your own community and beyond, and act on what you learn.

- **Live in Solidarity:** Our life circumstances may not allow us to live side-by-side with those we meet in mission. Our focus becomes living at home in a way that honors those we meet during our experience. Find ways to stay connected to the people you met and the issues you learned about. Live with a renewed understanding that we are one human family.

- **Work for Justice:** Our experiences in mission help us to understand justice and peace in new ways. Find ways to stand with those who suffer injustice and to work for change in your own community and beyond.

- **Be an Advocate:** Solidarity moves us to advocate on behalf of those we meet in mission and the issues that affect their lives. Perhaps the most important thing we can do for those we meet is to be a bridge to this culture that has so much influence in the world.

- **Remain Faithful:** Integration is continuing to practice what we learned and living the values we witnessed. Allow your experience to influence your lifestyle, commitments, relationships, and how you use your time and resources.

- **Live Mission at Home:** Living the call to mission is not about going far away. It's about being the hands and feet of Christ every day, wherever you are.

You may have returned home from your mission experience feeling transformed and motivated to make changes. It's easy to be enthusiastic about the experience and what it means to you when you first return. Remaining faithful to what the experience taught you may be challenging over time, especially if others around you don't share your commitments. It will be important to find others who share your vision, beliefs, and values.

If your family and friends were not part of the experience they may not share your feelings. Without seeing firsthand what you witnessed, they may not understand you. Some may even be shocked, feel judged, or appear defensive in response to what you share. Integration is not a sudden thing. It takes time for the meaning of the experience to emerge. It will be important to share the thoughts, feelings, and ideas that surface over time with those closest to you. They may never really understand. Any changes you want to make will mean more if your family and friends understand and support you in your commitment to live your beliefs.

> *My mission of being in the heart of the people is not just a part of my life or a badge I can take off; it is not an "extra" or just another moment in life. Instead, it is something I cannot uproot from my being without destroying my very self. I am a mission on this earth; that is the reason why I am here in this world. We have to regard ourselves as sealed, even branded, by this mission of bringing light, blessing, enlivening, raising up, healing and freeing. All around us we begin to see nurses with soul, teachers with soul, politicians with soul, people who have chosen deep down to be with others and for others. But once we separate our work from our private lives, everything turns gray and we will always be seeking recognition or asserting our needs. We stop being a people.*

— Pope Francis, *Joy of the Gospel*, #273

Reflection Questions

How does the Pope Francis quote help you to understand integration?

_____

_____

_____

_____

_____

_____

How does your program support the importance of integration?

_____

_____

_____

_____

_____

_____

How will you help the members of your group explore what "I'll never be the same" means for them?

_____

_____

_____

_____

_____

_____

How can you help the members of your group to live mission at home? What programs exist in your parish and community that members of your group can get involved in when they return from the experience?

_____

_____

_____

_____

_____

_____

Chapter 4
Tool Kit for Reflection

This Tool Kit provides leaders of short-term mission experiences practical ideas to use during each phase of the missioning process. The sample activities and reflection questions found here can be used as they are written or modified to meet the needs of your group. Hopefully these examples will inspire you to create your own activities for your group.

Preparation Phase

1. Individual Discernment

The discernment and selection process is key to the short-term mission group. Inviting God to be part of choosing who is right for this experience at this time is important, especially if what the group is truly about is being an instrument of God's love. The following questions can be used to assist potential group members and leaders with the discernment process.

Step 1: Self Reflection

• What motivates (or moves) me to want to do this?

• What are possible subconscious motivations?

• What have I done in my life that I feel the best about? Which of my qualities made it possible?

• What makes me come alive and energizes me?

• What are my strengths and talents? How have I shared them for the good of others?

• What are my weaknesses? How have I worked to address these?

• Do I have the faith, commitment, maturity, willingness, health, experience, or skills that are needed for this experience? Why do I feel this way?

• What will be the greatest challenges for me? How can I deal with them?

• How do I feel about offering myself, about being present to those who are poor or suffering in ways I've never experienced before?

• What values and beliefs mean the most in my life?

• Who will be affected by this choice?

• Do I have the qualities and maturity to do this, with this group?

• Is this time the best timing for me to do this?

• Is this the best choice I can make?

Step 2: Connecting With God

• Who is God for me?

• How and when have I experienced God's presence?

• What has been the most surprising way God has spoken to me? Through what events? What experiences? What persons?

• What, specifically, do I reveal about God to others? How have I known God's power working in me and through me?

• How do I practice my faith? (prayer, meditation, sacraments, worship, scripture, service, etc.)

• In what ways will I connect with God in order to hear God's message for me?

• How and when have I felt called by God in my life?

• In what kind of matters have I sought God's guidance? How has the result surprised me, if it did?

- Have I had the experience of thinking that I was being led by God to do something, and it turned out *not* to be so? What were the consequences? Looking back on it, what might have alerted me to this?
- Have I ever used "God's will" as a cover for my own plans or ideas? Am I doing so now? What led me to do it?

Step 3: Making the Decision

- Who are my discernment partners who will accompany me in this discernment process?
- In discernment it is important to be choosing between two or more possibilities. What are the possibilities that I am considering at this time?
- What have I done so far to discern whether this is right for me?
- What is attractive about this decision (pros)?
- What is unsettling (cons)?
- What are my criteria for saying yes to this experience?
- What is my priority?
- What have I heard about this program that makes me want to be part of it? What have I heard that doesn't feel right for me? What do I need more information about or time to think about?
- What have I learned from my past experience with discernment and decision-making? How will I put this learning into practice in this situation?
- Is this the best time for this choice?
- How would this be consistent with my life?
- How would this be different than my life choices so far?

Step 4: Confirming the Decision

- Do I experience peace in reflecting on this choice?
- Is my heart at home in this possibility?
- What does my body tell me about this choice?
- How is this consistent with what I believe and have done previously?
- Does this fit what I want to do with my life?
- What do those who know me best say about this decision?
- Do I truly believe that this is what God wants for me?

Confirmation of our decisions continues as we proceed through each stage of the preparation process. With each presentation, conversation, and prayer opportunity, it is important to continue to ask, "Is this right for me?" After each encounter consider the following questions:

- What did I hear or what struck me that stays with me?
- What continues to resonate with me? Why?
- What does not resonate with me? Why?
- How is my heart feeling? Does it tell me something about me? Does it tell me something about this group?

There is a wonderful feeling that comes with believing that we are following God's will.

2. Sending Group Leaders' Discernment

Is this person ready for this type of experience at this time?

- What is his/her motivation for participating?
- Do I believe this person is emotionally and spiritually mature enough for this experience?
- How has she/he demonstrated readiness?
- What concerns do I have?
- Is there something that could happen during the preparation process that would help me feel better about their participating in the group?

Is this person good for the group?

- Of what other groups is this person a part?
- How have they reacted to what is expected of the group?
- What have I seen when this person interacts with the others in the group, with the leaders, presenters, or those we have been in service to during the preparation process?
- How has this person contributed to a sense of community?

Is this person right for the people where we are going?

- How does this person demonstrate the following qualities that are important when encountering the poor, another culture, anyone:
  - faith;
  - courage;
  - compassion;
  - respect;
  - sensitivity;
  - presence.
- What is their experience of moving out of their comfort zone?
- What is their experience with another culture?

As the leader...

- What am I doing to be faithful to the discernment process?
- What am I doing to support my own faith life?
- Who/what supports me as leader of this group?
- What do I need to do to make the best choices for this group?

3. Group Covenant

- Ask each person to identify: what I need; what I offer; what the group offers. Consider talking, listening, learning, understanding, spirituality, decisions, conflict, support, time alone, time with group, hopes, fears, other.
- Identify and discuss any similarities and differences.
- Ask the group to write statements on how they want to act, to be treated, and to work together around these areas. This is the basis for the group covenant.

4. A Conflict Resolution Technique

- Identify the problem. Be honest.
- Focus on the problem. The goal should be to resolve conflict fairly.
- Attack the problem, not the person. Come up with options to resolve the conflict. Choose what works best for all.
- Listen with an open mind, without being judgmental, accusatory, or demeaning; without interruption. Be willing to put yourself in the other person's shoes. Be willing to admit you are wrong.
- Treat a person's feelings with respect.
- Take responsibility for your actions; carry out agreements and commitments.

5. 9 Questions

During each phase of the missioning process, consider using the questions developed by Tim Dearborn in *Short-Term Missions Workbook*. Using these same questions will help participants to identify how their perspectives have changed with the experience. The questions include:

1. Who am I? What can I learn about myself?
2. Who is God? What can I learn about God?
3. Who are we? What can I learn about community and the church?
4. What is the impact of culture on faith? How can I see life and the Gospel differently because of this experience?
5. What is wrong with the world? What can I learn about justice and poverty?
6. What does it mean to be a follower of Christ? What can I learn about discipleship?
7. What is of value? What can I learn about my lifestyle?
8. Where am I going? What can I learn about my vocation?

An additional question to consider is:

9. What is right with the world? What can I learn about joy, service, and love from others?

6. Sharing Your Concern

In two circles facing each other, answer the following questions. After each question the outside circle rotates one to the right so that each will share with someone new.

- What is one thing that breaks your heart when you see it?
- What brings tears of gratitude and joy to your eyes?
- If you could change one problem in the world, what would it be?
- Outside of your family, what is the most important thing you have ever done?
- When you look at all that Jesus did in his life, what is one thing you feel you have done to follow his example?
- Gandhi said, "My life is my message." What do you think has been your message so far? What would you like it to be in the future?

7. Openness, Presence, Transformation, Solidarity

Read about these components of mission (pages 12-13) and answer the following questions:

Openness

• When have you demonstrated openness in your life? What has been the benefit of being open?

• When have you not been open? What was the result?

• How do you feel about being open to receiving and learning from others? Why?

Presence

• What examples of presence have you seen or experienced in your life? What impact did it make?

• How do you feel about the focus being on "being with" versus "doing for"?

Transformation

• How would you describe transformation?

• What are examples of transformational moments from your life or the lives of others?

• How do you feel about being transformed by this experience?

Solidarity

• At this point in your life, with whom do you live in solidarity? In what ways do you live in solidarity?

• How do you feel about this experience calling you to live in solidarity with the people you will meet?

Overall Reflections

• Which of these four components will you find the most challenging? Why?

• Which of these components energize you?

• Using images, symbols, or words, demonstrate these four components.

8. Sisters on a Common Journey (submitted by Mike Haasl)

The following is an example of the beauty and importance of the dominant culture sharing pain that resulted in a much-deepened relationship. As part of a Global Solidarity Partnership between the Archdiocese of St. Paul-Minneapolis and the Dicoese of Kitui, Kenya, the Minnesota delegation visited Kenya. In a small group meeting with women from Kenya, Bonnie shared how her husband had died some twelve years earlier. Theresa told her: "When I came today, I couldn't see how I could possibly have anything in common with you visitors from the U.S., but now I know how. Your husband died in 1993, mine died in 1992. You know my story, you've worn my shoes, you have felt my pain." Bonnie and Theresa looked at each other, eye to eye, nose-to nose, and shook with tears of joy and knowing. They were sisters on a common journey, blessed to be in one another's company sharing stories of sorrow and joy, pain and resurrection.

• How do you see openness, presence, transformation, solidarity reflected in this story?

• What does this story say to you as you prepare for mission?

9. Giving and Receiving

In groups of three people, choose from the following questions and answer:

- What is the last thing you received? How did it feel to receive this?
- What is the last thing you gave? How did it feel to give this?
- When was the last time you received something that was totally unexpected?
- What is the greatest gift you could offer someone that is not a material possession?
- When do you find it hard to receive from someone?
- When do you find it hard to give to someone?
- What is one way that you could show you care, or be present to someone you do not know?
- How does someone receive graciously?
- Share a time when you felt "I received far more than I gave."

Each group presents to the large group any common responses shared. In the large group discuss the following:

- If you believe it you will see it.
- What do you think you could learn from the people you are going to serve, or from someone who lives a life of material poverty?
- Mission is mutual.

Think about a relationship that is mutual. What is good about mutuality? What would mutuality look like in a short-term experience?

10. A Ritual on Service and Presence

In pairs, take turns washing and drying each others' feet.

Use olive oil or massage oil to massage each others' feet.

Discuss:

- What was this experience like for you?
- What was it like to serve vs. to receive?
- What was the difference between the foot-washing and massaging with the oil?
- What is the message for us as we go out to others?
- What does this activity teach us about presence?

11. Let Us Work Together

Read the quote and discuss the questions that follow.

"If you have come here to help me, you are wasting your time .... But if you have come because your liberation is bound up with mine, then let us work together" (Lilla Watson, Aboriginal educator and activist).

- What is Lilla Watson telling us?
- How do you feel about this message as you approach this mission experience?
- How can you honor this message during this mission experience?

12. Impact and Outcomes

Ask each participant to express how they hope their presence will effect the people they will meet in the experience. Discuss the following questions, which may be new ideas to the participants:

- What are potential short and long-term impacts of mission travel on people living in the host country?
- What positive and negative effect could this experience have on the people there?
- How does the experience fit into your long-term mission goals and those of your hosts?
- What can the group do so that the impact is positive?
- How does the experience relate to local issues in which your group and the participants are or would be involved following the experience?
- How can this experience lead to a positive impact for your local community?

13. Artwork to Unpack our Thinking

Ask small groups to design posters, paintings, sketches, clay models, or other artwork to depict life in the developing world. When the groups are finished, facilitate a discussion in the large group using the following questions:

- Are the words and images mostly negative or positive?
- Why do you think this is?
- Where do we get our ideas and images of the developing world?
- How would you feel about being described like this by people from far away? Why?
- If an organization from Africa wanted to produce a poster depicting life in the U.S., what would you like to have shown on it?
- Ask the group to look for stories about the developing world from the national media. Are the stories positive or negative? Why is this? Compare this with information from development or mission groups.

14. Dialogue with Photos

Gather a collection of photos of people from different cultures in the world or from the culture you will visit. Lay the photos in the center of the group and ask the participants to spend time looking at them. Instruct each participant to select one photo that speaks to them in some way. Give a few minutes for each to look at the person in the photo. Ask each one to share:

- What do you think the person in the photo would want you to know about his/her life?
- What words of wisdom would this person give you as you prepare to go out to meet others through this experience?

15. Prayer Map

Place a large world map on the floor and sit around it. Place small candles all around the outside of the map. Invite each person to come forward and place a candle on a part of the world he/she would particularly like to pray for, name the place, and say what is happening there and why he/she wants to pray for it. When all have placed their candles, spend time in silence together. Conclude with a short prayer or reading.

16. Learning About the People and Culture

What is your present understanding about the site and people you will visit?

How did your understanding come to be?

How open are you to this understanding being challenged or changed?

What excites you about what you know?

What fears do you have?

Learn more about

- the history of the area;
- current issues challenging the area where you will go;
- the geography where you will be;
- uniqueness of the area;
- important people historically and currently; and
- significant moments in the history of the church there.

Besides doing research on the culture and history of the place where you will be going, it is helpful to talk to those who know that culture best, including

- the receiving group who will facilitate your experience;
- local people who are from the culture where you will go;
- former missioners who know the area; and
- peace and justice groups.

Consider attending a church service of a cultural or language group that is similar to the one you will be visiting, or a culture other than your own to experience what it is like to be different.

17. Who Am I?

A big part of any cross-cultural experience is learning about ourselves and our own culture. To help participants start to become more aware of their own culture, have each give 10 responses to the following prompt and then discuss in large or small groups.

- *I am ...*

18. Self Portrait

Using pictures, symbols, or words, have the participants illustrate who they think people see when they first meet them, or what people think they are like. Draw who they want people to see or who people will see after they get to know them. Discuss in pairs, then in the larger group.

Discuss what to remember as they approach people of another culture.

19. Respecting Cultures

Read the following quote and discuss the questions that follow.

"The world in which you were born is just one model of reality. Other cultures are not failed attempts at being you. They are unique manifestations of the human spirit" (Wade Davis).

- What does Wade Davis mean when he writes, "Other cultures are not failed attempts at being you"?
- What actions, behaviors, or comments would demonstrate this attitude?
- What can the group do to show respect for the culture where they will go?

20. Cross-Cultural Communication??? (submitted by Mike Haasl)

One of the most important and overlooked aspects of cross-cultural relationships is that of culture and the challenges of intercultural cultural communication. This may be best highlighted by a brief narrative. Marty, a missioner who had returned from the Sudan, shared how shortly after he arrived at his place in the Sudan he asked a woman on the road, "Is this the way to the market?" The Sudanese woman politely told him, "Yes, it is." Marty walked on for quite some time, not finding the market. He eventually realized that he must have been given "false" information. He was confused about what he was told, but later he was told by another missioner: "Africans are very relational. It means everything. For a Sudanese to tell you 'no,' it might have been construed as disrespectful, a way of weakening the relationship. If you would have asked, 'Which way is it to the market?' you would have been given the correct direction. In Africa, sometimes 'yes' means 'no'! It can take a long time to figure out when 'yes' means yes and when it means no."

- What will be important to remember when communicating with people from a culture different from your own?
- What do you think you can do so that your situation is not like Marty's?

A suggested resource for cross-cultural communication is *The Wolf Shall Dwell with the Lamb: A Spirituality for Leadership in a Multicultural Community* by Eric Law.

21. Take off Your Shoes

Read the following quote and discuss the questions that follow:

"Our first task in approaching another people, another culture, another religion is to take off our shoes, for the place we are approaching is holy; else we find ourselves treading on someone's dream. More serious still, we may forget that God was already there before our arrival" (John Taylor, *The Primal Vision*).

- What are examples of how your group can "take off your shoes" in this experience?
- What might the people to whom you will go "dream" of?
- What are ways to see and experience that "God was there before your arrival"?

22. Justice

- Ask participants to identify a situation or policy in their home community that they think is socially unjust.
- Engage in a discussion about the difference between an unfair policy and a policy they do not "like."
- Discuss what form of direct action might make a difference, such as a letter writing campaign, boycott, picket line, informational brochures, or other form of advocacy.
- Discuss the pros and cons of different forms of protest and action.

23. Catholic Social Teaching (CST)

Divide the group into small groups and give each group one of the principles of Catholic Social Teaching (CST):

1. Life is sacred, and the dignity of every human person is to be respected.
2. All people are equal and have the right and duty to participate fully in the life of their community.
3. All people have human rights and also must be challenged to live up to human responsibilities.
4. We are called to emulate God by showing a special preference for those who are poor and weak.
5. We work to continue the construction of God's Reign on earth.
6. We belong to a global family and are challenged to love our neighbor as ourselves and to be in solidarity with our sisters and brothers around the globe.
7. We share one planet; we are stewards of God's earth and all of creation.

Using words or images on a poster, have each group present:

- How the world's reality differs from that value. For example: CST Principle: Life is sacred, and the dignity of every human person is to be respected. Words or images might include: capital punishment, abuse of women and children.
- Examples of people or organizations that are positive examples of this value and what they do.

24. A Parable (by Brian Wren)

There was once a factory that employed thousands of people. Its production line was a miracle of modern engineering, turning out thousands of machines a day. But the factory had a high accident rate. Day after day, men and women came out of work with squashed fingers, cuts, bruises. Occasionally someone was electrocuted or crushed to death.

Enlightened people began to see that something needed to be done. First on the scene were the churches. An enterprising minister organized a small first-aid tent outside the factory gate. Soon, with the backing of local parishes, it grew into a properly built clinic, able to treat quite serious cases. The local Rotary Club and Chamber of Commerce then became interested and the clinic grew into a small hospital, with modern equipment, an operating room and a full-time staff of doctors and nurses. Several lives were saved. Finally, the factory management, seeing the good that was being done and wishing to prove itself enlightened, gave the hospital its official backing and a small annual grant. It also donated an ambulance to speed serious cases from the workshop to the hospital.

But, year by year, as production increased, the accident rate continued to rise. More and more men and women were hurt or maimed despite everything the hospital could do. Only then did some people begin to ask if it was enough to treat people's injuries, while leaving untouched the machinery that caused them.

- Did the churches do the right thing in the first place? Later on?

- What would you advise the churches to do now? The factory management? The factory workers?

- What does this parable say about the churches and politics? About charity? What parallels can you draw with other situations you know about?

- How do you feel about the points the parable is making?

- What is the message for our group?

25. Stories of Good Intentions (submitted by Mike Haasl)

Recent history is replete with well-intentioned but failed programs designed by those who are more educated and economically well-off trying to "help" those who are "less fortunate," because they didn't know or pay attention to the culture, and/or they didn't engage with the local culture (except as a means to effect the change). What's worse, however, are those instances when the lack of cultural or local or even global understanding, has led to putting vulnerable people into an even more risky situation, all done in the name of "helping."

- In the early 1980's in rural Kenya, as part of a "development program," I was encouraging small farmers to put a portion of their land towards growing coffee, which would increase the cash they could generate. In order to participate and get credits with the cooperative, they had to put an entire acre into the program, nearly half of the size of many of the small farms. When I mentioned this to a missionary priest, he immediately asked, "What happens if the price of coffee drops on the world market?" I was stunned. I hadn't even considered this possibility. I quickly realized to my horror that I was actually potentially contributing to the demise of the very people (who risked putting their scarce land which had been growing subsistence crops into cash crops) who I had sincerely thought I was "helping."

- Sometimes things which might seem like an obvious way to "help," might cause breakdown in the social fabric and thereby detract from the very help that was intended. For example, an outside group wanted to "help" by putting in a water system to alleviate the struggle of local people walking distances to the community water source to get their daily water. But it turned out that that local water source was the place of daily gathering, where community relationships were nurtured and the social fabric was strengthened, and so the water program inadvertently resulted in weakened relationships. Another obvious example is the case of giving some benefit to one or a few members of the community, thereby setting up jealousy among those who didn't benefit. What was meant to help resulted in the opposite effect.

Does this mean we should not act at all? Not necessarily, but these examples do point to the need to be attentive to the many dimensions of the lives of the people that we want to "help," including their local community, their culture, and the various social structures (local, national, and international) in which they are immersed. It means spending time walking with the people, carefully listening to them and their hopes. It may at times mean opening up opportunities for them that will lead to a fuller, sustainable life, but it also ought to mean being able recognize, reflect upon, and offer potential negative consequences of any change that they decide upon.

- What questions do we need to ask ourselves so that our actions do not hurt more than help?
- How do we find out what the people want and need before we act?

26. Commissioning

A ritual marking the commissioning and departure of the short-term mission group may be celebrated with the community sending the group and who will be represented by the group. This may be a prayer service or preferably a ritual during community worship, as close to departure as possible. The ritual might include elements such as

- calling each person in the group by name and using the symbols of baptism—water, oil, candles—to remind her/him that each is called to mission through baptism:

  −sprinkle the participants and all gathered with the water;

  −anoint each with oil; and/or

  −give each a candle;

- blessing the hands and feet of each as a reminder that they are the hands and feet of Jesus Christ in the world;

- using any scripture, prayers, quotes, or group mission statement that has been chosen as the theme of the experience. Possible scripture quotes can be found in "Understanding Mission" (see page 10);

- during the final blessing ask each gathered to raise their hands or gather around and lay hands upon the participants to bless those who go out in their name.

INSERTION PHASE

1. 9 Questions

Continue to use the 9 Questions exercise on page 77 throughout the experience and then again after your return to demonstrate what has been changed by this experience.

2. Journal Writing

Journal writing can be an important part of helping participants look at the experience, express their feelings about what is happening, and record it so that it can be looked at after the experience. Remember that not everyone likes to journal, so provide a variety of ways people can express themselves, such as artwork, drawing, and conversation. Consider the following:

- Prepare different sheets for each day of the experience (in different colors, with the date) with three questions for each day. (See the list of questions under #3 below for more questions.) For example:

  – What do I remember from the day?

  – How do I feel about what happened today or about this experience?

  – How did I experience God today?

- 5-Minute Write: Give participants 5 minutes to write about a subject that will be discussed in the large group.

- Graffiti: Ask participants to express what they are feeling or thinking about a certain issue by using graffiti (a mixture of symbols and words). If possible, provide paper and markers or colored pencils. Discuss in pairs, small groups, or large group.

3. Daily Check-ins

On a regular basis, ask participants to discuss and/or journal about the experience. Consider questions such as:

- Who or what was significant today?

- What did you learn from them?

- What image stands out?

- What was said that was important?

- How were you challenged?

- What has been difficult today?

- What feelings seem to keep surfacing for you in this experience?

- Why do you think this experience/situation initiates these feelings?

- How does the world look different today?

- What signs of hope do you see?

- What problems have become more obvious?

- What does this teach about your own culture?

- How do you see God present in this situation?

- What might God be saying to you through this?

- What are you learning?

- Ask each participant to choose someone from the experience and reflect on what it would be like to be that person.

4. Bible Study Model

- Describe the situation or identify the issue they are facing.

- Reflect on Scripture passages that address this issue. Based on these passages, what do you think God's message is for us?

- Reflect on your response. What does God ask us to do?

5. Learning About the People

An important way to learn about people is through observation. Instruct participants to observe the following questions and discuss with a cultural guide or someone who understands the culture. Ask yourself the same questions about your own culture.

- How do they worship?

- How do they relate to God?

- How do they relate to each other?

- How do they relate to Earth?

- How do they relate to themselves?

6. Observe–Judge–Act Model of Reflection

(from the Office of Social Justice, Archdiocese of St. Paul and Minneapolis)

Observe

- What do you know about this issue or what did you observe?

- What specific facts can you cite about this issue or experience? What did you learn or observe?

- How do you feel in the face of this issue or experience? How does it touch you personally?

Judge

- Social Analysis

  Why does this situation exist? What are the root causes?

- Economic Factors

  Who owns? Who controls? Who pays? Who gets? Who gets left out? Why?

- Political Factors

  Who decides? For whom do they decide? How do decisions get made? Who is left out of the process? Why?

- Social Factors

  Who is left out? Who is included? Why?

- Historical Factors

  What past events influence this situation today?

- Cultural Factors

    What values are evident? What do people believe in? Who influences what people believe?

- Theological Reflection

    What lessons or values from scripture can help us interpret this experience?

    What key principles of Catholic Social Teaching apply?

Act

- Do you have enough information and analysis to act? If not, what additional research is needed?

- If you were to act to change this situation, what root causes would you attack? How would you transform the structures and relationships that produce this situation?

- How can you act to support the empowerment of those who are poor or disadvantaged?

7. Catholic Social Teaching (CST)

Remind the group of the Principles of Catholic Social Teaching (see page 83). During group processing ask group members to share examples they witnessed during the experience:

- Where does the local reality not honor these values?

- What people or organizations are working to support these values and the actions that demonstrate these values?

8. But Why?

If we really want to make a difference in a lasting way, we need to look deeply at the root causes of the problems we encounter. One way of doing that is to use a process called *But Why?*, in which we ask this simple question repeatedly in order to understand a situation more deeply. The following example illustrates how this questioning process takes us deeper into understanding an issue:

- I saw a person picking through the garbage cans. *But why?*

- He was looking for aluminum cans. *But why?*

- So he could sell the cans. *But why?*

- He needed money to buy food. *But why?*

- He doesn't have a job. *But why?*

- Because the steel mill closed down. *But why?*

- Car companies decided to buy steel made in another country. *But why?*

- So they could make more profit. *But why?*

When you reach a question you cannot answer, this is a place to do additional research, study, and personal reflection. It also offers an opportunity to consider ways in which I might be called to engage directly with this issue by taking specific action.

9. Evaluation

Evaluation is an important part of any experience. Consider asking the participants to respond to some of the following prompts, either in their journals or in group conversation.

- The thing I liked best about my experience was...

- The thing that made my experience most unpleasant was...

- What I learned from this program was...

- The highlight of our time was...

- The area in my life where I saw the greatest change was...

- The thing I'm most thankful to God for is...

- What difference has this program made for me?

- How do I sense this program will help me as I continue my journey of faith?

- What is one thing I will do as a result of this program?

- What suggestions would I make for future experiences?

- The biggest challenge I face in returning home will be...

- How do you anticipate your life being different after you return home?

- How would you complete this sentence in 25 words or less? This mission experience for me was ...

10. Re-Commissioning to Mission at Home

The experience comes to an end. We say our goodbyes and return home to reflect on the lessons learned through this experience. Consider at your final group gathering to use this "re-commissioning" service, taken from *Remaining Faithful: A Guide for Reflecting on Short-Term Mission Experiences*, to help remind participants that mission does not end when we return home. God calls us to live mission in a new way because of this experience.

Prayer of Sending Forth

Finally, my sisters and brothers, your thoughts should be wholly directed to all that is true, all that deserves respect, all that is honest, pure, decent, admirable, virtuous, or worthy of praise. Live according to what you have learned and accepted, what you have heard me say and seen me do. Then, will the God of peace be with you (Phil 4:8-9).

Questions for Reflection or Group Sharing

- What will you always remember from this experience?

- Who are the people you are most grateful for from this experience?

- What are the gifts of your journey?

- How are you different because of this experience?

- What is one way that you will continue to live mission when you return home?

- What would you like to say to the others in this group?

Prayers of Petition

I ask God's blessing for ...

I ask God's healing and peace for...

I thank God for ...

Re-Commissioning

Bless one another by tracing a cross on the forehead, ears, eyes, lips, heart, hands, and feet as directed in the following prayer:

Receive the sign of the cross ...

... on your forehead. It is Jesus Christ who strengthens you with this sign of love.

... on your ears, that you may hear and be guided by the voice of God.

... on your eyes, that you may see the glory of God every day of your life.

... on your lips, that you may speak of God's justice, peace, and love.

... over your heart, that the Spirit of God may dwell there.

... on your hands, that Jesus Christ may be known in the work you do.

... on your feet, that you may walk in the way of Jesus Christ.

As you go, remember to live simply, love generously, serve faithfully, speak truthfully, act peacefully, remember constantly, pray daily, and leave the rest to God.

RETURN PHASE

The Need for Reflection

Many people do not understand the importance of continuing to gather and look at the experience after it is over. Integration of the experience requires reflection. Consider using the following quotes when explaining the importance of reflection.

> *Experience is not the best teacher. We learn nothing from experience. We only learn from reflection on the experience* (Tony Saddington).

> *Experience without reflection is not learning* (Paulo Freire).

We offer a book to guide this process. *Remaining Faithful: A Guide for Reflecting on Short Term Mission Experiences* is a manual for reflection, integration, and prayer after a short-term experience in another culture. Use the book as a companion to *Understanding Short-Term Mission* to help your short-term mission participants process their experience.

Remaining Faithful includes:

- what to do when you return from your experience;
- understanding your feelings and lessons learned;
- themes for reflection and prayer after your experience;
- resources to assist with reflection and integration.

Find out more about *Remaining Faithful* at **www.missiontomission.org**.

Post-Trip Gatherings

Groups are strongly encouraged to meet after returning home, to continue to support each other and to reflect on and pray about the experience together. The amount of time given to the return phase will vary from group to group. We suggest using *Remaining Faithful* to assist you with reflecting on the mission experience. If you do not use *Remaining Faithful*, the following are suggestions for one or more post-trip gatherings.

1. Prayer

- Continue to use prayers, quotes, songs, or scriptures that were used throughout the experience.
- Pray for the concerns of those met during the experience, for the world, or for the local community.
- Pray in thanksgiving for those met during the experience, for the group, the supporters of the group, and anything participants became aware of through this experience.
- Pray for guidance and strength for living mission here at home.

2. Check-in

- Since returning, to whom has it been easy to talk? To whom has it been difficult to talk? Why?
- Has the trip changed you? Why or why not? If so, how?
- What thoughts or memories keep surfacing?

3. Share Photographs

As you look at your photos, what people, events, moments stand out for you? Why do you think that is?

4. 9 Questions

Return to the questions on page 77 one last time. Answer these questions and then compare the answers written before and during the experience.

5. A Reflection Model (from Amor en Acción)

Describe the most critical incident of the experience, the "high point" or "low point" of the mission experience. Describe it as best you can, including your feelings about the situation. If it was a "low point," attempt to state the problem as you see it. If it was a "high point," state why. If it was a "low point," list other ways you might have handled it. If it was a "high point," state any new insights or growth you perceive in the situation.

- Where was God in this incident for you?
- What feelings are surfacing in you from this experience?
- Why do you think this experience/situation initiates these feelings?
- What signs of hope do you see?
- What problems do you see?
- What do you think are the causes for hope, or the lack of it, which you experienced?
- What do you think may need to change in the future in your attitude, lifestyle, and approach related to the global issues raised by this experience?

6. Reviewing Social Analysis

In small groups, review issues raised during the experience and post-trip sessions. Identify how individuals and groups were responding to issues of poverty, and put those responses into one of the categories identified by Boff and Boff (*Introducing Liberation Theology*, 1986 Orbis Books)—aid, reform, liberation.

Aid

- offered by individuals moved by the spectacle of widespread destitution
- a "band aid" approach
- treats the current situation
- the poor are seen as collective objects of charity
- fails to see that the poor are oppressed and made poor by others
- does not address root causes
- increases the dependence of the poor

Reform

- improves the situation of the poor, but always within existing social relationships and the basic structuring of society

Liberation

- a strategy to change social conditions
- the oppressed come together, come to understand their situation through a process of conscientization, organize themselves, act in a coordinated fashion
- transforms the society in the direction of a new society

Discuss the following questions:

- What were the positive models that you saw in action?
- What did they actually "do" that made it a positive model?
- What does this teach us about how to respond to the needs of the poor?

7. Catholic Social Teaching (CST)

Remind the group of the Principles of CST (see page 83). Have participants form small groups to design a poster. Using words and images from the mission experience, create a poster of what CST looks like (both positive and negative) in that reality. Present them to the group.

Ask the participants to reflect on and share answers to the following questions:

- What have you learned about CST through this mission experience?
- How do you feel about CST being part of what it means to be Catholic?
- Which principle do you think is most needed where you visited? In this local community? In the world?
- Which principle has become more important to you through this experience?
- How do you see CST as a part of mission?
- How will CST be part of your life in the future?

8. Staying Connected (from *Remaining Faithful*)

Stay connected to your experience and values through:

- **Prayer and spirituality:** Bring your care and concerns to God.
- **Stories:** Identify a few stories that illustrate key moments of learning from your experience that you can share when an opportunity arises.
- **Reminders:** Find a place in your life for art, crafts, photos, music, and food that remind you of your short-term experience.
- **Network and community:** Find others who share your values, beliefs, and lifestyle, as well as organizations that focus on issues about which you feel most passionate.
- **Be informed about world and local justice issues:** Stay educated about the issues in your community, the area you visited, and beyond.
- **Connect with social teaching:** Research what your faith community teaches about social justice and practice it.
- **Life-long learning:** Continue to be open to learning, new ideas and different ways to do things.
- **Live values learned:** Live in a way that honors the people you met during your short-term experience and what you learned.

- **Intentional living:** Be conscious of your values in the way you live each day and in how you make decisions.
- **Conscious choices:** Before making purchases, consider whether it is something you need or want; read labels on your food and clothing to see where and how they were made; whenever possible buy fair-trade goods and environmentally responsible goods.
- **Meaningful action:** Find work or involvement that reflects your values and helps you feel that you are making a positive contribution to the world.
- **When faith becomes passion, things change:** Motivated by faith and reflection, together with others who share your vision, do something to positively impact issues that concern you.

9. Living Simply

Witnessing poverty through a mission experience can be very challenging for participants. Many begin to question their lifestyle and may choose to live more simply at home, but do not know where to begin. A good place to start is to be mindful of our consumer practices.

Review the following checklist and discuss how each would impact living more simply.

Checklist for consumers trying to live more simply:

- Do I really need it?
- Can I really afford it?
- Will it enrich my quality of life or that of others?
- Is it worth the time and money to store, clean, otherwise maintain?
- How many hours will I have to work to pay for it?
- Could I borrow it from a friend, neighbor, or family member?
- Is there anything I already own I could possibly use instead?
- Are the resources that went into it renewable?
- Is the product socially and environmentally friendly?
- Can I recycle it when I am through with it, or will it help clog a landfill?
- Were the workers who made this treated fairly?

10. Solidarity (from Matt Rousso)

- Solidarity is about
  - binding ourselves to the poor and oppressed;
  - attitude (be-attitude);
  - acting, about doing something;
  - the cause of the poor—not just their condition; and
  - a long-term relationship.
- Make a list of possible solidarity actions that could be engaged in on behalf of the people you went to be with. This includes actions you have taken, actions that you heard about that others are engaged in, actions that you have started thinking about as a result of your participation in this program.
- Which one(s) of these actions seems most appropriate for you personally? Where do you sense God might be calling you? What do you think you would like to commit to here at home?

Act of Dedication

Jesus' call to follow him into fullness of life is not an easy or comfortable one. Sometimes the thought of all that might be involved can paralyze us into doing nothing. God does not call us and then leave us to get on with it. We are called to do what we can, where we are, one step at a time.

Ask each to reflect on the following:

- What is the next step God is calling you to?
- Write a resolution, however small, you feel able to make that will enable you to respond more authentically to God in your life.
- Bring the resolutions to the altar or prayer table as a sign of commitment to God and God's people. We do this believing that God will accept and bless our efforts.

You want me?
Here I am.
Learn from me.
Be with me.
Support me.
You know my name now.
Listen to me.
Talk to me.
Advocate for me.

When you came to me, I opened your eyes.
When you made time for me, I opened your mind.
When your heart cried out as you prayed for my injustice,
I changed your soul.

Thank you for loving me the way you have.
And know that I am not far away even though you are back.
You still see me every day on the street,
and I am embedded in your heart like never before.

Keep choosing to act on your love for me,
and I will save your life.

— Bruce Bachmeier, Passionist Volunteers International (Jamaica)

Catholic Teaching on Mission and Justice

Documents of the Catholic Church: **www.vatican.va**

Ad Gentes: On the Mission Activity of the Church

Gaudium et Spes: The Church in the Modern World

Evangelii Nuntiandi: On Evangelization in the Modern World

Redemptoris Missio: On the Permanent Validity of the Church's Missionary Mandate

Centesimus Annus: A Century of Social Teaching

Evangelii Gaudium: The Joy of the Gospel

Laudato Si': On Care for Our Common Home

Statements from the U.S. Catholic Bishops: **www.usccb.org**

To the Ends of the Earth: A Pastoral Statement on World Mission

Teaching the Spirit of Mission Ad Gentes: Continuing Pentecost Today

Called to Global Solidarity: International Challenges for U.S. Parishes

Communities of Salt and Light: Reflections on the Social Mission of the Parish

Everyday Christianity: To Hunger and Thirst for Justice

Sharing Catholic Social Teaching: Challenges and Directions

From Mission to Mission **Services**

From Mission to Mission offers support to returning missioners, volunteers, and their sending organizations in the following ways:

Re-entry Workshops

Since 1980, intercultural missioners and volunteers have found the **From Mission to Mission** workshops a valuable part of their transition process. We offer two Re-entry Workshop formats for returning missioners and volunteers, a 10-day Workshop and a Weekend Workshop. Our workshops provide a safe place where missioners and volunteers are understood. The workshops focus on:

- Telling the story of the mission experience;
- Honoring the gifts of the experience;
- Recognizing what needs to be healed from the experience;
- Understanding re-entry and transition; and
- Integrating the mission experience.

Re-entry Resources

From Mission to Mission offers the following books for sale through our website:

Returning Home: A Guide for Missioners and Volunteers in Transition

Welcoming Them Home: A Guide for Families and Friends of Returning Missioners and Volunteers

Finding Life After Trauma: A Guide for Missioners and Volunteers and Those Who Care for Them

Remaining Faithful: A Guide for Reflecting on Short-Term Mission Experiences

Understanding Short-Term Mission: A Guide for Leaders and Participants

Consultation

From Mission to Mission staff is available to offer support and advice to individual missioners, volunteers, and mission sending communities and organizations at any phase of the mission experience—before, during, or after.

missiontomission.org

About the Author

Julie Lupien has been the Executive Director of **From Mission to Mission** since 2002. In 2015, she received the first Pope Francis Mission Award from the U.S. Catholic Mission Association, in recognition for years of excellence, vision, and compassion while ministering to missioners returning to the United States after both long-term and short-term mission engagements. As a member of the Volunteer Missionary Movement (VMM) Julie served in Zimbabwe, Africa, and St. Kitts, West Indies. Julie's short-term mission experience includes Alternative Spring Break in Appalachia when she was a campus minister at Northern Illinois University, participating in the Young Neighbors in Action program in Yakima, Washington, and a parish mission trip to St. Kitts when she served as a Pastoral Team member at Spirit of Peace Catholic Community in Longmont, Colorado.